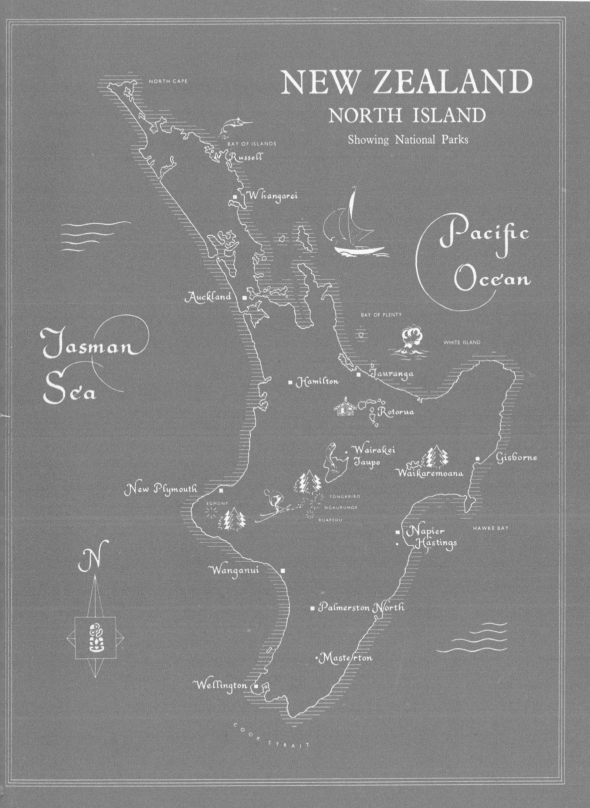

NEW ZEALAND
NORTH ISLAND
Showing National Parks

NORTH CAPE

BAY OF ISLANDS

Russell

■ Whangarei

Pacific

Ocean

Jasman
Sea

Auckland ■

BAY OF PLENTY

WHITE ISLAND

□ Tauranga

■ Hamilton

Rotorua

• Wairakei
Taupo

Waikaremoana

■ Gisborne

New Plymouth

EGMONT

TONGARIRO
NGAURUHOE
RUAPEHU

HAWKE BAY

■ Napier
Hastings

N

Wanganui ■

■ Palmerston North

•Masterton

Wellington □

C O O K   S T R A I T

NEW ZEALAND

KENNETH MELVIN

NEW ZEALAND

"The Small Utopia"

COLLINS
P.O. BOX No. 1 AUCKLAND
1962

TO ENA

FOREWORD

New Zealand is a land of infinite variety and whoever sets out to enclose that variety within the covers of a book engages in a complex and difficult task.

All the preliminary work which goes into the production of a book such as this – the research, the compilation, the correlation, the checking and the balanced selection of information, illustrations and statistics – can be lost if the author then fails to present his conclusions in readable form. Happily, Mr. Melvin has handled his material with smooth dexterity and a sure touch which holds the reader's interest while imparting a wealth of information.

The task has been accomplished with great success. This book is a most valuable addition to the literature dealing with New Zealand and it appears at a time when there is more need than ever before for this country to make itself known and appreciated.

THE HON. D. J. EYRE,
Minister in Charge of Tourist and Health Resorts

CONTENTS

PREFACE

The Small Utopia

"Let there be a small country, with small population
Where the supply of goods is tenfold or hundredfold more than they can use:
Let the people value their lives and not migrate far.
Though armour and weapons exist, there is no occasion to display them.
Let them enjoy their food, beautify their clothing, be satisfied with their homes,
*   delight in their customs;*
Needing never to move outside their own country."

'The Book of Tao': II–LXXX: Laotse
c. 604–531 B.C. translated by K. C. Lee

Blue-prints for the ideal society, from Plato down to the confused contemporary dreams of internationalism, have always been excursions into the improbable.

Yet here in New Zealand, some 2,400 years after Laotse, we have a country which seems to conform closely to his prescription for Utopia. The Chinese sage might even approve our rare New Zealand greenstone, which is a nephrite jade.

Visitors usually find in this country that which they seek – a new experience in travel; a group of Pacific islands on the rim of the world, air-conditioned by the surrounding ocean, with scenic grandeurs unique in their variety, accessibility and quietude even at the height of the season.

But New Zealand is much more than an oasis in the tourist circuit. Here, in convenient capsule form may be observed bold and often pioneer achievements in social welfare, for New Zealand has been extraordinarily successful in establishing the greatest good for the greatest number of its people.

The truth about it all may be difficult to find in a visitor's full schedule, but at least it does not lie at the bottom of a wishing well. New Zealand is very much a going concern, playing a full part in the world community, interdependent with other nations yet following an independent course towards democratic ideals. It might have been for us that Thomas Jefferson wrote: 'It is neither wealth nor splendour, but tranquillity and occupation which give happiness.' Visitors with the means to travel so far are likely to have many better things back home. But if it is important that the good life be shared by all, then something significant is under way in New Zealand.

The purpose of this book is to introduce us not as a lotus-land, but as a young nation distinguished by its degree of social security, equality of opportunity and general prosperity. Indeed, so tranquillised has New Zealand been said to be that we are prepared to be told that even our cows are more ruminative than elsewhere!

We shall not insist that New Zealand was created by Providence for the edification of the wider world. It is permissible to question the all-ascendancy of our way of life. But 'a map of the world that does not include Utopia is not worth even glancing at, for it leaves out the one country at which Humanity is always landing.'

LET THERE BE A SMALL COUNTRY . . .

THESE ISLANDS lie so remote and detached in the South Pacific Ocean as to seem on the maps a mere matchstick in a bucket of water. In fact, they are roughly the size of Britain, and like Gaul they divide handily into three parts; three central islands, whose total area is one-third in sown pastures and crops, one-third in marginal grasslands or commercial forest, and one-third in mountain country.

By continental standards, everything is small except the mountains. The largest city has less than half a million people, there are only 15 urban areas of more than 20,000 and only 4 with more than 100,000. Almost half of all the farms are of less than 100 acres, the average dairy herd is about 50 cows and the average sheep flock about 1,100. The total labour force is less than a million, and the 8,600 registered factories employ fewer than a fifth of a million people. Of every 20 workers, 4 take part in primary production, 7 are in other industries and the remaining 9 provide services; a high proportion which reflects both the advanced organisation and the standard of living of New Zealanders.

Comfortably within the south temperate zone, the country is luxuriantly evergreen, so favoured by soil, sunshine and rainfall as to be able to turn grass into livestock more cheaply than other countries. The farmlands, where grass grows year round, are fully electrified and mechanised, so that all but a few of the two million cows are machine-milked and practically every major operation of the 90,000 farms of all types – dairy, sheep and mixed – is performed with machines.

New Zealand is thus the world's chief exporter of dairy products, ranks second in wool exports (its sheep population is the third largest, excluding the U.S.S.R.), and is increasingly an exporter of newsprint. This prosperity is divided among fewer than $2\frac{1}{2}$ million people.

Because it is one of the smallest of the democracies, with its population lightly scattered at about 20 to the square mile and producing such astonishing quantities of farm and forest products, New Zealanders occupy 'a small house in a large garden'.

If affairs in Lilliput are naturally better regulated than in Brobdingnag, we need look no further for the explanation of this country's distinctive character and performance. There is,however, more to it than that.

Switzerland is also a small democracy, and the visitor to New Zealand finds in our countryside many delighted recollections of the Confederation; superb alpine panoramas of peaks, snowfields and glaciers, mountain sports, fishing, health resorts and spas.

The differences between the two countries are not only that Switzerland has twice the population in one-sixth the area, is more heavily industrialised, has three nationalities, four languages, an oddly archaic political federalism and many centuries of history. What most distinguishes New Zealand from Switzerland is that the latter has chosen neutralism in a world whose peace and prosperity are indivisible.

New Zealand has paid the full price of admission to the world community.

Throughout this century New Zealand has been a fully committed partner of the free nations. It fought from beginning to end of the world wars, and as a member of the British Commonwealth and of the United Nations, it participates in the responsibilities of collective security. It is a signatory to a Treaty with the United States and Australia, and is a member of the South East Asia Treaty Organisation. Substantial and continuing contributions are made to the welfare of Asian peoples through the economic and technical aid programmes of the Colombo Plan. This country has afforded refuge for displaced persons from Europe, opening to them full British nationality, and also numbers among its new citizens settlers from the Netherlands and other parts of Northern and Western Europe. But the population has remained throughout our growth predominantly and staunchly British.

Colonised in the 19th century flood of radical idealism, this country illustrates the timeless truth that man and soil flourish – or decline – together. The simple economics of husbandry, administered by the politics of equality, have produced a welfare society that comes uncommonly close to the ideal. In New Zealand may be found something of Massingham's aspiration; a community in which nature, husbandry, religion and the home can combine in peaceful prosperity and national healthiness.

When migration to an untried country takes place, the physically weak and the timid tend to stay at home. The strong, the intelligent,

8

and those with initiative are likely to go furthest. New Zealand is the most distant land which Europeans have settled; before they came, the Maoris crossed the vast Pacific in frail, open canoes. The achievements of New Zealanders, European and Maori alike, can be attributed in great part to this early process of selection. As Carl Sandburg says of the American trek westward; "The cowards never started and the weak ones died on the way."

The search for social and economic welfare has gone well in these islands because we have escaped the cult of bigness. Lacking any special strategic importance and without major resources of oil, iron, or precious metals, New Zealand has been passed over in the 20th century struggle for place, power and prestige.

In the evolution of European society, 'the cities, their commerce and manufactures, instead of being the effect have been the cause and occasion of the improvement and cultivation of the countryside.' In contrast, New Zealand has been able to follow the natural order, directing the greater part of its capital and labour first to agriculture, and only afterwards to manufacture and commerce. As a result we are not afflicted by the mischievous relic of feudal thought that agriculture is an inferior occupation, with the accompanying class distinction between those who labour and those who lead.

What is even more to the point, New Zealand has gone on to develop its grasslands management by applied science as the broad base of the national economy. Thereupon has been built much of our industry and therein lies the explanation of our social unity.

Unburdened by great possessions, unimportant in power politics, and therefore unentered in the arms race, New Zealanders can live secure in the knowledge that a fifth of our people and a third of our production centres are not likely to be destroyed between nightfall and sunrise.

All success is compounded of good luck and good management. New Zealand is no exception.

2

. . . WITH A SMALL POPULATION

THIS IS a comparatively empty land. In an area upon which Great Britain sustains 50 million people and Japan 95 million, New Zealand can muster fewer than 3 million. That sort of comparison provokes questions as to New Zealand's right to hold so sparsely a country which is so manifestly capable of greater population and diversity of production. The best answer New Zealanders can advance to date is that our forefathers were its first settlers after the Maori migrations; in three generations we have made it one of the world's most advanced countries, and in three wars we have defended the right of all peoples to self-determination.

Economic planning in New Zealand is closely related to social welfare, and it has long been held that our living standards, our traditions and our institutions would suffer under any large-scale influx of aliens. Therefore, a controlled population growth has been an important element in our planning. Racially, we are the most homogeneous of any British country, with over 90 per cent of the people being of British descent and with less than 2 per cent born in foreign lands. Our selective immigration policy has therefore been framed to preserve the Anglo-Saxon society which we drew from the Mother Country.

New Zealand reached its first million of population in 68 years, its second million 44 years later, and the third is expected some 20 years after that, in 1972. This will be a 50 per cent increase in a single generation. In a recent 5-year period, this country's rate of increase was 11 per cent compared with 10 per cent in Japan and the Netherlands. In a list of 21 countries New Zealand shows the fourth highest rate of population increase, a growth that can be accommodated at our existing standards only by controlling the population.

The strength of our small population has lain in the natural wealth of primary production under our favoured circumstances. We sell food, wool and forest products, and buy manufactures, producer materials, and components for assembly. Nor has the growth of new and more diverse industries greatly altered our dependence upon reciprocal trade. New Zealand does not possess many raw materials that would support a high concentration of people in industrial processing. We are now developing what we have, but scarcely to the reversal of our traditional economic bias. Ours is therefore a dependent economy needing careful direction and regulation.

Any more rapid increase in our numbers could not be absorbed in primary production, so that it must focus chiefly upon urban centres of manufacturing. There have long been more workers in factories than on the land, and factory employment and production have doubled over the last quarter-century. The central problem in New Zealand has therefore been to keep town and country in balance and both within prudent expansion.

Our manufacturing industries were first established in the seaport cities at which raw materials could be landed close to services and a sizeable labour pool. More recently the inland provincial cities have increased their proportion of industrial occupation, a dispersion of industry that has prevented the emergence of the Satanic mills and dormitory slumdom of the all-too-familiar pattern. New Zealand has not needed the mass-production methods of continental countries. Our cities already sprawl unmanageably, with more than enough noise, smog, clotted transport, urban congestion, economic waste and decadence. That our problems have so far assumed but trifling proportions compared with the great metropolitan centres of the world is both a warning and a guide.

It is perhaps New Zealand's best achievement to have re-enthroned human values in a community able to satisfy all sensible material needs without incurring the worst excesses of the affluent society.

Our very smallness has spared us the dehumanising effects and neglect of personal values that seem to accompany great city concentrations. The health and wellbeing of New Zealanders can scarcely be enhanced by the mere multiplication of people, things and wants.

Our relations with the native people whose land and life we have civilised are probably as near to equality and fraternity as can be found in this imperfect world. Fundamental issues between the two races don't arise, though they have been manufactured. The characteristics of the Maori – good humour, kindliness and intelligence have greatly eased and accelerated their assimilation. Yet again this has been possible because the Maori people constitute only some 7 per cent of the total population amongst whom they are unsegregated, protected landowners, with equal entry into all walks of life and an equal capacity to profit by it. Generally speaking, they are at their best in rural communities where they have good living conditions, high earning capacity and a valued place in the local football teams. Such discrimination as still exists is social rather than racial, for the Maori is not grimly ambitious; his easy-going ways tend to stabilise around simple creature comforts, though of course distinguished exceptions arise in all callings. The Maori population, once declining alarmingly, now doubles every 20 years, twice the rate of European New Zealanders; a trend in no way discouraged by the universal State family-benefit for all dependent children.

Those with a point to make can prove that despite all the legis-lative guarantees of racial equality, the Maori is still indubitably a Maori; though it is difficult to see how this is a reproach to either race. All Maori scholars and leaders are not agreed that the wisest policy lies in progressive adaptation of their people to European life and institutions; but these are academic considerations beside the drift citywards into substandard dwellings and aimless entertainment which is what usually happens to the Europeanised native. It is this – the gravitation of the Maori people themselves – that defeats the aspiration of both races for their social betterment: on the one hand governmental provisions for education, housing and welfare services; on the other hand, Maori leadership with its gospel of work, health and self-discipline.

Whatever ancient resentments may linger from the wars and dispossession of pioneer days, the four Maori Members of Parliament can ponder the poetic justice which periodically gives them the balance of power between the two political parties.

New Zealand is a simple, direct, representative democracy in which the people look to the politicians to stop the rot. If they don't, we can change the Government every three years. Our politicians know the rules, and are men of unsuspected shrewdness who have learned that the business of government is to rectify, and that it never did consist in writing on a clean sheet of paper. Somebody else has always written on it when you get it.

For a quarter of a century there has been a continuity of policy undisturbed by the pendulum of politics, directed to the development and improvement of a welfare society whose numbers are manageable, whose needs are calculable and whose demands are predictable. At any given time, roughly half the population will be willing to testify that the Government is a Genghis Khan with telegraphs (since each party is about equally supported and both are prisoners of the high-tax programme). The cynics will say that it is all very much a matter of Tweedledum-Tweedledee, and that when the parties go at it triennially with their pots and pans, whatever happens it will be the mixture as before—no great rewards for anybody but small prizes for all. The most prosperous will insist that State-controlled capitalism is a euphemism for a gloved thumb on the windpipe. With neither rich nor poor, they ask, where is the spur?

The facts hardly square with this view. Over the last decade or so there has been comparative peace in industry, with few strikes and virtually no unemployment; with total national income, salaries and wages rising five-fold, share-values climbing steadily, capital investment out-pacing the available labour and with sustained increase in the supply of goods and services. Taxation has increased over the period, sixfold. The politician answers this final statistic by pointing out that so long as taxation policy is an instrument for the redistribution of the national wealth through the extension of social security benefits, then the people are getting exactly what they ordered.

The fate of governments in New Zealand never turns upon great international issues or upon fundamental changes in social objectives. It is possible for a small population to be singularly agreed upon a policy of current expenditure. So it is always the little more or the little less in taxation and provisions; always the reform of reforms, never their repeal. Our small and single-minded community is always very close to its political representatives and under our short-term Parliaments recall is direct, frequent, and salutary.

New Zealand long ago decided that one of the most important functions of the State is to prevent extreme inequalities of fortune. So we have few pawnbrokers and fewer millionaires. The relation of the New Zealander to the State is an interesting one. He is far less suspicious of State activity than the American or the Western European is said to be, and if government cannot stop the rain it can at least supply an umbrella. It is a simple matter of history and topography. Older countries have long memories of tyranny and oppression to which New Zealand has never been subjected. That is the historical factor. The topographical one is in the spread of a small population over a thousand miles of often difficult terrain with scattered towns and isolated farmsteads that never would have essential services unless they were centrally planned and financed. State activity was therefore inevitable where there was little private finance, and there is no dark history to document the dangers of too much centralised control.

Our best intelligences may rail at what they describe as the disquieting uniformity imposed by State provisions over so many aspects of society, but the advantages have been so direct and tangible for our people as to outweigh any potential dangers.

*   *   *   *

No rural population enjoys more of the amenities of life than does the New Zealand farmer. Sheep raisers receive the highest average income in the country, followed by dentists, doctors, business men and lawyers. There is an emerging rivalry between town and country, between a traditionally agrarian economy and the newer manufacturing industries, for first claim on government consideration. But New Zealand as one of the world's great pastoral countries, can scarcely be in doubt regarding a specialisation in occupations that enables so few people to win so much from the good earth at so little economic cost.

Like their kindred everywhere, New Zealand farmers most truly reflect the national character. Though there are more townsmen they owe more to outside influences. Of the 20 million acres capable of cultivation by plough or disc, something like two-thirds are owned by their occupiers. Yet the farm population is only about one sixth of our total numbers. They are therefore a minority playing a major role with all due independence of mind and purpose. Those who like to say that joint-stock Capitalism and Socialist bureaucracy have between them extinguished individual freedom don't know the New Zealand farmer !

He has no great respect for anything but good husbandry, no great scorn for anything but ill-thrift. The craftmanship of the saddlemaker and the shearer, the farrier, fencer and farm-mechanic is likely to be more conscientious than that of the production-line townsman. The man on the land works hard, but he is no drudging peasant. Mechanisation has removed the back-breaking toil. On many a farm broken-in by the last generation with a horse and a dray-full of slashers, the son droves sheep in a Jaguar. The bulk of sheep-shearing is done by machine-clippers, with which a good man will take 300 fleeces a day. Aerial topdressing, pioneered in this country and used here more extensively than elsewhere, has enabled many a high-country farmer to double his wool-clip in five years.

Over the last quarter-century there has been a decrease in the numbers working on our farms, yet production has increased by 50 per cent, through farmer-scientist co-operation, better farming techniques and increased mechanisation. New Zealand has long had the world's highest per capita farm production and the most scientific pasture-management.

The wider world is rapidly changing from a society predominantly agrarian to one predominantly industrial. The importance of the New Zealand farmer is not only that he has anchored the country against a shift so inappropriate to our economy, but also that he demonstrates that nothing – even in the space-age – can outrank in importance the efficient, lowcost production of food, clothing and shelter. It is almost as though our farmers knew that quite apart from these timeless needs,

15

one-third of the world's vital raw materials for industry now comes from agriculture and forest products.

When they are embattled, as they have been and doubtless will be again, it is a good thing for New Zealand that their shouts are heard round the land; and when they are cosseted as they currently are, it is still a good thing. For New Zealand's essential struggle is with living things – the earth and the growth it sustains; forests, pastures, crops and livestock. It is therefore in the rural communities that the visitor will find the characteristic New Zealander. If this paragon seems disappointingly sober in dress, thought and speech, it were well to remember that the English language is richest of all in monosyllables – something that suits the New Zealand farmer down to the ground.

3

WHERE THE SUPPLY OF GOODS IS TENFOLD OR HUNDREDFOLD MORE THAN THEY CAN USE

MAINTAINING a production-surplus that is desirable, marketable and profitable is quite a trick. The way New Zealand does it demonstrates the importance of choosing the right forbears, the right country to be born in and the value of every man to his trade.

New Zealand and the United Kingdom each produces best what the other needs most, so Britain buys over half of our exports and sells us about half of our imports. Outside the British Commonwealth, the United States and France have been our next best customers, and we have commercial dealings with nearly every trading country in the world. By specialising in the surplus production of staple commodities New Zealand has always had a market abroad, and if in the matter of price, realisation does not always come up to expectation, this is a phenomenon not confined to trade. In hard times, national kinship has belied the counting-house maxim that there's no sentiment in business.

Thus by prudent management, family loyalties and mutual support, New Zealand has been able to make the best of its natural advantages without recourse to the desperate expedients of soil banks, antic stockpiling, surplus dumping or sheer wealth destruction. In a world of competition this country is anything but poorly placed.

New Zealanders themselves consume record quantities of the protective foods we produce in such abundance: a per capita average of 43 pounds of butter, 230 pounds of meat and 337 pints of dairy milk per annum. According to the United Nations Food and Agricultural Organisation Tables, New Zealand has one of the highest daily food-intakes of calories per person in the world; and New Zealand leads in the percentage of food from animal sources, having the highest per capita consumption of milk products. But when we have done our best, the great bulk of national production still remains for export: two-thirds of the meat, four-fifths of the butter, nine-tenths of the cheese, and nineteen-twentieths of the wool-clip. This constitutes three-quarters of the total world exports of mutton and lamb, and the largest national export of butter and cheese. On our farms, more than 290 pounds of butter-fat per cow is the annual norm, rising to 350 pounds on the best pastures. To this output is added hides and skins, condensed and powdered milk, apples and pears, canned and quick-frozen fruits and vegetables.

Some 47 million sheep yielding 550 million pounds of wool per annum gives us an average of $11\frac{1}{2}$ pounds per sheep – a quarter more than the figure for the United States. A century ago, the wool-clip averaged $2\frac{1}{2}$ pounds per sheep; by the middle of the 80's the figure had doubled, and now it has doubled again by selective breeding, pasture management and animal husbandry. This latter has developed a most profitable sideline in the pure-breeding of sheep, cattle and horses, by which New Zealand has periodically produced more than half of all the purebred livestock exports in the world. In the process, we have of course vastly increased the worth and yield of our own flocks and herds. The export revenue from hides and skins is roughly one-tenth that of the wool-clip.

The other major source of New Zealand's wealth comes from our forests, which cover nearly a quarter of the land. Whilst waiting for the slow-growing indigenous forest to regenerate after milling, nearly a million acres of exotic trees are maturing at twice the rate they would in their native lands overseas, growing at an estimated rate of 10,000 tons every 24 hours and thereby posing a problem of sheer embarrassment of riches. Over the last two decades their utilisation has brought spectacular growth in our pulp and paper industries so that they are becoming of world importance and have attracted overseas interests with ample finance for their expansion. New Zealand is thus a significant exporter of raw materials for newsprint, pulp, paper, timber and building materials.

On all these counts this country has one of the world's highest levels of trade per head of population, exporting over two-fifths in value of total production. It is upon this agreeable basis that we have been able to pursue sustained national development in all our industries, services and institutions. The efficiency of it all is shown by the fact that though primary industries engage only some 15 per cent of our labour force, they yield more than 50 per cent of the total value of goods produced and provide more than 90 per cent of the country's exports! This rather makes nonsense of the modern theory that only a self-sufficient industrialisation can provide for an advanced society.

Of the two typical views as to the future of such a small-population high-production economy, the one falls short and the other goes too far, so that the truth is straddled.

Some would like to think that reciprocal trade with our protected British markets holds the key to perpetual prosperity, with New Zealand secure in its basic farming, agricultural exports, restricted immigration and leisurely light industries for home consumption – a safe social democracy insulated from the 20th century industrial revolution. With an impressive standard of living, full employment, social security applied on a lavish scale and a paternal State providing everything from free medical attention and baby bonuses to betting services for the horse races, why should New Zealand embark upon major industrial expansion? For one thing, the argument runs, plants catering for a few million people cannot effect mass-production economies except in a few specialised industries. For another, major population increase with more intense urbanisation and industrial concentration could only weaken our traditional trading relationships. The resultant changes would make New Zealand a bigger nation but would it be a better?

On this case it is held that the country could at most support at present living standards only six to eight million people in an economy that would merely make the worst of both worlds by being neither efficiently agrarian nor industrial. Therefore it would be wiser to rely upon natural population increase gradually accommodated without undue stresses within much the same trading structure as has served us so well.

The other view is that New Zealand's purely farm economy, efficient though it is, cannot provide the basis for growth in numbers and gross national production that is required if the country is to keep pace with either its own or the world's rate of growth. The pattern of the world market for our limited range of products has altered. The Ottawa Agreements as protective Commonwealth measures are outdated, so that between 1953 and 1958 the proportion of New Zealand goods sold to the United Kingdom fell from 67 per cent to 56 per cent, while the proportion going to the United States rose from 8 per cent to 15 per cent. In 1938 the United Kingdom took 84 per cent of New Zealand's exports: by 1958 this had fallen to 56 per cent. Trade has been opening with many foreign countries, so that New Zealand is moving outside its traditional orbit and should exploit the rapid increase in world population and world trade. Thus we should go out to meet the changing future by relaxing our immigration laws, aiming at ten to twelve millions as soon as may be, directing the bulk of our capital resources, and all from abroad that we can attract, into industries that will reduce our propensity to import and thus participate in this greatest economic expansion in the history of the world.

It is anticipated that by the end of the century, even without accelerated immigration, New Zealand will have doubled its present population. Then consuming twice the present proportion of its primary production, and needing twice the quantity of imports, we will find ourselves on a very different economic footing. On this basis we must increasingly make for ourselves many of the commodities we now import, building our new industries on the manufacture of the raw materials which New Zealand itself produces. With our labour force increasing at the average rate of 20,000 per annum for the next 20 years, to state the problem is to define the answer – a high rate of growth lifting us from the status of a small agrarian nation into diverse and heavy industrialisation.

Both these views give insufficient consideration to the all-important factor of the welfare system of New Zealand, which raises large questions for both the static and the expanding society. The one cannot hope to sustain welfare at present levels, and the other can hope to improve it only under carefully controlled conditions. Because we have 'tenfold or a hundredfold more goods than we can use', export trade must continue to be our chief business; and because expenditure on social services, monetary social security benefits and subsidies now absorb half the proceeds of taxation, such standards can be sustained and improved only by steadily increasing production on all fronts. The determinative word, however, is 'steadily'. The demands of the Welfare Society leave a volume of savings too low to support a high rate of growth. But all welfare provisions are an investment in human capital – in better labour – and the mounting volume of foreign capital may be adequate, though it has lately been only between 2 and 3 per cent of national income.

What the New Zealand people will not contemplate is the curtailment of the Welfare Society which is the very essence of our national life. It would be political suicide for any Government in this country to attempt its undoing. Changes there must be, but they will be required within the existing framework of the planned society.

*   *   *   *

The first great surge in New Zealand's development occurred with the invention of refrigeration, which brought a vast new market for our butter and cheese no less than mutton and lamb. By 1921 their combined export value had actually surpassed that of wool. Scientific dairying had changed the whole context of our farming so that the muddied, toiling 'cow cocky' began to share the rewards in income and leisure hitherto confined to the 'gentleman sheep farmer'. Since then, wool has again taken the lead over meat by a narrow margin, with dairy produce a lagging third. In 1959 a new American market for beef pushed meat once more ahead of wool in export value.

In between these changing leads, the years 1957-1958 saw an alarming fall in our export prices and national purchasing power abroad, so that we took our eyes off the runners and saw the obstacles they all had to surmount. Today, we are more dependent upon the big three – dairy products, meat and wool – than we were 25 years ago, all of them unstable in price. This situation is dangerous because in these years New Zealand has been building a Welfare System that cannot hope to ignore serious economic reverses. In that last recession, New Zealand's defences proved to be sufficient, and the country has recovered. But it is now too hazardous for us to rely upon these three items for the bulk of our national income.

In so far as industrial diversification will erect safeguards against transmitted troubles, the case for it seems unanswerable, despite any lingering longing to live on in the comfortable Cockaigne of the past. Already, the utilisation of forest products, the projected oil production, iron and aluminium smelting, with extensions in the textile industries and in the manufacture of vehicle components and stationary engines show the pace at which this country is expanding. Even if capital be forthcoming from abroad, there is still much to be done in developing the requisite technical skills.

All this represents a second great surge, this time in new directions. Up to 1939, New Zealand was roughly at the same stage of development as was the United States before its industrial expansion after the Civil War. There was a substantial textile and leather-goods industry, we produced most of our furniture and building materials, manufactured many of our farm implements, assembled most of our cars and household appliances and processed most of our own food. The printing and metal industries, and the soap and confectionery trades were growing steadily.

During the war, when a large measure of self-sufficiency was forced upon so isolated a country, an unexpected variety of goods was produced, much of it to precision standards. Chronometers, aviation equipment, petrol engines, timber jacks, barbed wire, fire pumps, mortars and winches were among the light industrial output; and mine sweepers, launches, steel oil-barges and training aircraft demonstrated that heavier industrial production was even then within our competence.

But such small-scale operations could not survive the resumption after the war of competitive trade. Even though it had been shown that 'New Zealand can make it', it just did not pay to keep on doing so in the face of superior, lower-priced imports. In any case, if we did not buy neither could we sell, and so it was accepted that the artificial conditions of wartime had proved little that was relevant to the future. It was thought that the availability of imported raw materials was so directly conditioned by the balance of trade that New Zealand should stick to its last.

Since then our population has risen by 50 per cent, the postwar boom has surged and subsided, we have had recurrent crises in the balance of payments and we have found the inherent limitations of import licensing as a corrective; so that our best economic advisers seem agreed that we face a new and different era. Since the people have declared themselves repeatedly as requiring the maintenance of welfare provisions, the determining factor in New Zealand's future must be our willingness to abandon the illusion that governmental contrivances can be a substitute for fresh productive effort and creative growth.

It is in this second stage of national development that the Welfare Society will be fully tested. Apart from the national services of communication, transport, electricity and low-cost housing, New Zealand's industry is in the hands of private enterprise. Because it is firmly controlled by social objectives, this country is not without success in making the best of central planning. We certainly do not lack regulation of means to socially desirable ends. In defence of our economic security stand the Reserve Bank, the State owned Trading Bank of New Zealand, the establishment of the State as a major employer, and the devices of exchange, import and price controls.

It is not an open question whether New Zealand is to have greater industrialisation; that is already under way. What is an open question is whether we can have the blessings without the curses of concentrated industrialism. Will the processes of our growth tip the balance away from human welfare? Will it be for better or for worse, for richer or for poorer, for sickness or for health?

We need not anticipate the worst. It takes time and great determination to create human ant-heaps in dreary smoke-filled towns, squalid tenements and asphalt jungles. Such horrors in any case seem impossible in New Zealand's garden cities, clear blue sky and clean sea air. We are expanding after – not before – the Factory Act, the Arbitration and Conciliation Act, and the Town Planning Act. Here again we are able to follow the natural order: first the establishment of human welfare programmes, then the development of an industrial society.

What makes this the most stimulating period in all New Zealand's history is that there are no precedents for what we have to do. No other nation has the same set of circumstances – benevolent Nature, primary wealth, unity of social purpose, all the democratic freedoms, few of the world's great fears. No nation has more of its future in its own hands.

4

LET THE PEOPLE VALUE THEIR LIVES

FEW COUNTRIES can equal New Zealand's record in its human welfare programmes. With a death-rate that is one-third of the birth-rate, the expectation of life for the New Zealander is 68.3 years for males and 72.4 for females, figures that are bettered only by some Scandinavian countries. Pre-natal and confinement services are highly efficient and are a charge on the Social Security Fund, which subsidises all doctors' fees and private hospital treatment while public hospital services including X-ray and innoculation treatment are universal and free. A family benefit is paid for every dependent child sufficient to cover on the average the cost of its food, and there is free milk in primary schools and physical education in all schools. Cash benefits are payable at retirement with a means test at 60, or universal superannuation without means test at 65. There are pensions for widows, orphans and those disabled in war service, and payments are made to unemployed and to wage-earners incapacitated through accident or sickness. Almost all pharmaceutical medicines are provided free under the State medical scheme.

Mortality in early childhood, and especially in infancy, is considered to be one of the main indications of the social and economic level of a community. This is because most of the causes of infant mortality can be found within the normal conditions of family care and the mortality rate indicates the presence or absence of proper ante-natal care, maternity services, and proper home management.

The United Nations Population Studies recording the services given to mothers and children show that, over the last fifty years, no country in the world has been able to match New Zealand's achievement. Recently Sweden has established the lowest infant mortality rate, aided by a very low birth-rate, a rapidly ageing population and lax

23

abortion laws. New Zealand, with an increasing population and a high birth-rate, together with strict anti-abortion laws, retains its unequalled record for child care.

In general amenities New Zealanders are afforded the essentials of comfortable living, with a motor vehicle for every 3 persons and a motor-car for every 5 (a density exceeded only in the United States and Canada) a telephone and radio for every 4 persons, a refrigerator and washing machine for every 8. Three homes in every five have both a refrigerator and a washing machine, and 80 per cent of all homes use electricity or gas for cooking. New Zealand has long operated such advanced equipment as automatic telephone exchanges and is now among the first countries to instal electronic exchange systems.

The annual rate of home-building in this country is 8 for every thousand people, one of the world's highest but still insufficient for the demand of a nation of home-builders and owners. Over 80 per cent of all houses now built are for private home-ownership, and the average number of persons per dwelling is 3.5. Half the housing in recent years has been in the low-cost field, either financed through the State Advances Corporation or built by the State Housing Division for lease to lower-income groups, who have latterly been encouraged to purchase their homes outright. The quality of State housing is high and some of the best sites in the country have been selected for settlements. The State is by no means the only agency in low-cost housing though it is the largest, and this, like other welfare provisions, has been criticised for its subsidised basis. With the steady rise of general prosperity State housing would taper off were it not for the high building costs. It therefore continues as one of the important elements in the country's welfare programmes.

Within this broad context there is in New Zealand a strong sense of the legitimacy of government as an economic regulator to agreed social ideals. Controversy as to particular provisions is unceasing and often acrimonious, but it is by general consent that the State operates over areas of activity which in other countries are jealously reserved for private enterprise. So the Government, with about 12 per cent of the labour force is by far the largest employer, taking and spending the largest slice of the national income. It provides electric power, coal, forest resources, banking, insurance, transport, and communications. Of these only the last under-taking is a State monopoly, and in important areas of the marketing of primary produce there has been of recent years a systematic devolution of control to private enterprise.

Why has New Zealand accepted State activity more completely than for example, Britain, whose influence and traditions have been so strong in this country? It began as a matter of necessity. This land was colonised by men and women richer in faith than in capital, so that its early development had to be financed by overseas capital loaned to the New Zealand government – the only borrower acceptable to the lenders. Thus while other communities were using their own accumulated private capital, New Zealand had to rely upon State capitalism. This is a condition which tends to perpetuate itself unless there is rapid and sufficient increase in both population and savings to offset it. Neither condition arose in New Zealand. The natural consequence of all this has been a necessary reliance upon central government. To keep this situation in perspective it should be remembered that the London County Council controls and centrally administers a population much larger than that of New Zealand.

The soundest criticism that can be made of this Statism is not that it is wrong in principle, or that there is incompetence in high places. Neither is true in generalisation. Rather do we face the inherent limitations of bureaucracy anywhere. For the New Zealander, centralised control, with its traditional defects, is preferable to the uncertainties, poverty and inequalities of earlier, haphazard days.

*   *   *   *

The easy label for New Zealand is 'socialist', a tag made meaningless by its indiscriminate application to societies as dissimilar as those of Soviet Russia, Great Britain, and the United States under the New Deal programmes.

Historically, New Zealand's welfare legislation began in the 19th century liberalism which was brought to this country in somebody's sea chest and found to be just right for a new community unbothered by a past. The men, their motives and measures of reform have through the years been altogether too various for convenient tabloid explanation.

In 1891 the Liberal Party came to power upon the combined votes of land-hungry would-be farmers and the rising trade-union groups of the cities. After John Ballance, the great popular leader was bluff, self-educated Lancashire emigrant Richard Seddon. Anyone less doctrinaire could scarcely be imagined. It was during his ministry that New Zealand became in 1893 the first country to grant votes to women and in 1898 the second to set up a system of non-contributory old-age benefits. With Seddon's death in 1906, Liberalism lost its way and progressive legislation tapered off. There was the Worker's Compensation Act of 1908 covering incapacity by accident, the Widow's Pension Act of 1911, provision for the needy in 1912, for the blind in 1924 and the Family Allowances Act of 1926. But these measures were subject to terms so meagre and conditions so stringent that they were a reproach to the principles they affected to honour.

25

It was a cloud no bigger than a clenched fist – the 'recession' of 1928 – which blew up into the storm of the Slump of the early 30's that finally persuaded the New Zealand people to put up permanent shutters. Between 1928 and 1931 New Zealand's export prices fell more than 40 per cent, and the conservative Liberal-Reform coalition government could devise nothing more effective than dismissing civil servants wholesale, reducing government salaries and pensions, setting up made-work projects at sub-standard wages, suspending the safeguards of the Arbitration Court, raising the school entrance age and closing Teacher Training Colleges.

It was the cumulative effect of this bankruptcy of ideas that revived the militancy of labour and brought to office in 1935 the first Labour Government in New Zealand's history. By then, the nation was fully determined that this must never happen again. There was the same thinking all over the world, and it was from the logic of events rather than some doctrinaire creed that New Zealand embarked upon the Welfare Society. Australia had its first Labour Prime Minister as early as 1904, twenty years before Britain and thirty-one years before New Zealand, and their Labour Parties have been more radical. Yet neither they nor Sweden (which has been dominated by Labour for 30 years) matched New Zealand's recovery programmes.

If what was done in this country after the Depression was 'socialism' it was much more than a cranky creed. Before 1930, New Zealand had no unemployment insurance, sickness or invalidity benefits, free hospital treatment or medical scheme based on social security. For all the pioneer liberalism of the 90's, the country stumbled into the Depression without institutional or administrative defences. When it was all over and some retrospect was possible, no sensible reason could be found why this country should ever have been reduced to the penury of a relief camp. What was clear was that more would be needed for the future than sporadic and piecemeal measures which merely doffed their cap to principle without practical adequacy.

The concept of defence in depth against any recurrence of such disaster could only come from the extension of government into economic and social organisation. Other and less vulnerable countries might take their own courses. New Zealand went in for welfare by legislation.

It is true that throughout these formative years of the Welfare Society, both political parties have borrowed each other's clothes, to the cynic's delight but the country's comfort. This in itself shows that social welfare is in the warp and woof of New Zealand thought as a whole. The genius of the New Zealand people . . . no, let's restate that.

The vigour of our democratic system has evolved the Welfare Society as we have it, even if the political scientist may see it as more of a method than a philosophy. In New Zealand there is no Constitution needing to be kept up-to-date by tortured Court interpretations: there is no Bill of Rights whose glittering generalities can be as remote from daily living as is the solar system. But Professor William Graham Sumner would approve New Zealand's deference to his Forgotten Man 'delving away in patient industry, supporting his family, paying his taxes, casting his vote, maintaining the school and the church; the forgotten man who is not unseldom a woman'. The critics like to say that the underdog is debased by being made increasingly a ward of the State – whatever that may mean in practical terms. New Zealand has certainly made the handicapped and the under-privileged the first charge on the State accounts, but by universal provisions it is the man who pays the piper who has come into his own in this country.

New Zealand was one of the first countries to recognize that neither capitalist profit-sharing devices nor socialist rationing of wealth are in themselves sufficient for the healthy economy. What New Zealand has devised may elude precise political classification, but if it is State-regulated capitalism, it is nevertheless a thorough-going people's democracy.

*   *   *   *

The only legislative body in New Zealand is the House of Representatives, elected triennially on universal adult suffrage by secret ballot under every franchise safeguard. Since 1867 the House has included four Maori members elected directly by the Maori people. Over 90 per cent of the electorate usually vote in parliamentary elections. Of the two parties – National and Labour – that which wins the majority of the 80 electorates forms the Government, and its leader becomes Prime Minister, choosing his Cabinet from members of his party. Parliamentary debates are broadcast to the nation, affording citizens opportunity to know directly the arguments of both Government and Opposition on all major issues.

New Zealanders once seemed to fill Parliament with worthy men of full three score years, though opinions so differed as to whether they were in consequence the wisest and best among the good and the wise, that nowadays the average age-level is lower than it has ever been. A woman is customarily sought for the Welfare portfolios.

Local government devolves upon a clutch of minor bodies which shade off in importance from city, borough and county councils down to the last least rabbit boards, which by the administration of myxomatosis have reduced their voracious constituents to near-extinction. Apparently in the hope that they will go away, New Zealanders do their utmost to ignore these 981 local authorities, whose elections not uncommonly fail to arouse even 45 per cent of those entitled to vote. Despite Commissions of Inquiry into this rich realm of Parkinson's Law, our local authorities have resisted all attempts to reduce them in number, codify them in purpose or pacify them in temper.

It is at the national level, however, that the mainspring of the Welfare Society is wound by the hand of the electors, who in fact no less than in theory do control the controllers. As a people, New Zealanders lack the intellectual subtlety, the sense of history and the background of culture of older nations. But they yield to nobody in their ability to administer in politics the short sharp shock. To read the newspaper editorials one can only conclude that our governmental regulations are the most multitudinous, incommodious and vexatious on earth. Somehow, in the process, we have acquired a society in which communism has no talking points, trade unionism holds no terrors, race relations engender no hatred, religion is no bar to highest office, the judiciary is appointed for life (nor has it ever been necessary to remove a judge from office for malfeasance), the Courts are wholly free from political pressure, and the civil service is a career not at the pleasure of governments.

*　*　*　*

If there is one institution more than another which explains our way of life it must be our educational system.

Now that we are all democratically equal before the scythe of the tax-gatherer, the gate of opportunity, and the door of the infirmary, New Zealanders have turned demandingly to their schools to remedy the unfair distribution of brains. When anything arises to reflect upon us or to put our prosperity in doubt, it is the educational system that comes in for indignant scrutiny. Once, the cry was for more education, now it is for 'better', though any PTA meeting will demonstrate our democratic disunity as to what would in fact be a better schooling.

A former Minister of Education, Scots-born, was once persuaded to declare his policy, always a dangerous thing to do in a community as tendentious as ours. It was, he said, to build schools in New Zealand as England built churches - everywhere. He went on to explain that a young country so averse to Establishment and committed to free, universal and secular education had better make up its mind that other-worldliness could await enlightenment here below. He made the point that schools - if not churches - could be kept up to date.

As it turned out he was a good Minister, who not only saw to it that schools were built throughout the country and that the teaching

28

profession was rehabilitated after the rout of the Depression: he went on to become Prime Minister.

If a national education system is to say – rather than ask – what it should teach, and be judged by its general levels of attainment rather than by the brilliance of the few, then the ratios of our population graduating at the different stages support the United Nations' classification of New Zealand as among the best-read of all nations.

Our best graduates are good in any company. Limited opportunity, status and reward within the country tend to a flight of brains abroad, where our doctors, engineers, scientists and nurses are remarkably successful. When he retired after three decades as Warden of Rhodes House at the University of Oxford, Dr. C. K. Allen said that of all the Trust's world-wide constituencies, on balance New Zealand was the best. It was an opinion of our Rhodes Scholars shared by that eminent administrator and Rhodes Trustee, Rt. Hon. L.S. Amery.

Comparisons between national systems of education are largely pointless because each country must devise to its own special needs both the form and the content of its teaching. Nevertheless, New Zealand does have a higher proportion of university students than most other countries and more than any other British country. In a published list of 27 nations showing these statistics, the United States came first, Soviet Russia second, Japan third and New Zealand fourth, with Australia half-way down the list and Britain near the bottom.
In most New Zealand university degrees and diplomas, academic standards reflect a conscientious level of scholarship. Because our Universities are almost wholly dependent upon State finance they are scarcely the 'home of lost causes, forsaken beliefs and impossible loyalties'. Their task is chiefly utilitarian. We do not see much of bored young men fidgeting with their intellects or angry young men flogging dead horses. Whereas Great Britain has 29 Universities for its 50 million people, New Zealand has 4 Universities and 2 degree-granting agricultural colleges for less than $2\frac{1}{2}$ millions; an emphasis upon equality of opportunity which is the essential spirit of this country.

The New Zealander's attitude toward the educational system, through the successive stages of raw material, added value and finished product, veers over a wide compass, but he comes sooner or later to realise that he can become well-nigh anything he wishes to be. In this country there is no elite class and so no leisured learning. The drive for a living comes first, and if the pupils are not entranced by the prospect, the teachers are. Their path to promotion is paved with the skulls of scholarship boys, and the teachers' grading system requires close conformity to the syllabus upon which the national examination system crouches like a benign dragon. It aims at seeing that all have a general preparation for the inevitable, the majority acquire useful and marketable skills, and the talented few are challenged by sound academic standards.

The entire State system, from kindergarten through University is democratised: 87 per cent of all primary and 83 per cent of all secondary pupils pass through it. The remainder attend private schools maintained for the most part by religious denominations - Church of England, Roman Catholic, Presbyterian, Quaker and so on.

Governmental expenditure on national education over the last decade has trebled, and is now 4 percent of the national income; schooling is free - even to textbooks - till the age of nineteen, with university bursaries for all who qualify for entrance, even in the courses of medicine, engineering, dentistry and architecture. Its coverage of all New Zealand's youth is even and complete. If there are few schools that are superlatively good by continental standards of scholarship, there are none permitted to be dismally inefficient or unrelated to the business of living in this milieu. Standardisation is at once the strength and the weakness of our centralised system. Equality of educational opportunity has probably been more closely approximated in this country than anywhere else in the world.

5

THOUGH WEAPONS AND ARMOUR EXIST

THERE IS NO OCCASION TO DISPLAY THEM

SAFELY OBSCURE in a small corner of history and geography, New Zealand has no frontiers, colonies, territorial ambitions, military caste or standing army. Yet no country has been more promptly, consistently and unreservedly on the side of the angels in this century's resistance to military conquest. This characteristic of the New Zealand people stems from our origins, traditions and institutions. These alone were sufficient to bring New Zealand automatically to the side of the Mother Country in time of war. As a Colony, New Zealand grew into Dominion status under the protection of the British fleets, and so was spared the crippling costs of guarding on its own account some 4,000 miles of lonely coastline. Our national development has been financed chiefly from within the British Commonwealth. Our parliamentary democracy is modelled upon that of the United Kingdom from which we have drawn so much of our laws, literature and religious conviction. Above all, New Zealand is a self-governing constitutional monarchy, of which the Head of State is Her Majesty the Queen.

So this country was the first to support Great Britain against German militarism in 1914 and the first Dominion to capture enemy territory. From a population of little more than a million, New Zealand sent 100,000 men to overseas service, most of them volunteers; almost 17,000 lost their lives and 41,000 were wounded in campaigns throughout the Middle East and Europe. At home, the attenuated civilian population maintained an uninterrupted flow of foodstuffs for the Allied cause.

In 1936 this country supported Abyssinia and the policy of sanctions against Italy as the aggressor, not because the State of Abyssinia itself was worth the bones of a Pomeranian grenadier since it was the only slave-owning member of the League of Nations and its ruling junta maintained power by such barbarities as castrating rebels. New Zealand's spokesman at Geneva made it clear that his country defended the right of all peoples to self-determination in a context of collective security.

It was on this principle that New Zealand criticised the policy of non-intervention during the Spanish civil war, and supported the Chinese people in their appeal for aid against Japan, by prohibiting the export of scrap iron to the aggressor. In 1938 there was widespread opposition in New Zealand to the appeasement of Nazi Germany, even though we understood that Britain was thereby buying time to repair her defences. Although in all these crises we knew that ours was a small voice, we thought that it should be raised in our pledged support of democratic rights wherever they were imperilled. These principles again brought New Zealand into war in 1939 in defence of the freedom of Poland. This time, one-sixth of the entire population was under arms, and one out of every two males between the ages of 16 and 60 served in the armed forces. Throughout the Second World War, only Soviet Russia mobilised a higher proportion of its people. Once again, New Zealand stepped up its food production to Allied needs, and from the entry of the United States in 1941, this country became the main base for the South Pacific operations against Japan. At home, there was food rationing in order to release the maximum for the armed forces overseas.

New Zealand's conscription of wealth no less than her manpower took the form of heavy war-taxation which could reach a maximum rate of 90 per cent of the highest income brackets. Wartime excess profits were taxed by 75 per cent after other taxes had been levied. Compulsory war loans were floated, some bearing no interest for 3 years and a low rate thereafter. Inflation was checked by the imposition of rigorous controls on rents and the prices of some 40 items of food, clothing and public services. In short, New Zealand's entire resources were recruited throughout the conflict, in defence of political democracy abroad and social democracy at home.

When the United Nations intervened against aggression in Korea in 1950, New Zealand sent her armed forces and supporting services against the new form of tyranny. Our volunteer army and air forces have served in containing Communism in Malaya. Ours has thus been a full partnership in the free world community. Of all that this country enjoys, nothing is owed to abstention or neutrality.

Every generation of New Zealanders has known war at first hand: our own, against the Maori tribes in pioneer days; Britain's against South Africa at the turn of the century; the world's, against Nazism, Fascism and Communism. It is always difficult to assess the effects of war service upon a nation's youth. The office of a serving soldier is scarcely an ideal observation post, and from it the antiquity of Greece and Egypt, Rome and Florence is apt to appear only as the remnants of a decaying society. Two things however are clear in the New Zealand character; a detestation of war as an instrument of national policy, and a greater determination than ever to preserve and maintain our own form of political and social organisation. This is the hard core of the New Zealander's world outlook.

The Mother Country has never needed to understand because it has had only to accept gracefully the devotion of its smallest Dominion. But to the wider world beside which it has fought and endured, this country has given evidence of its independent maturity and responsibility. New Zealand therefore bears with composure the criticisms to which its way of life and political organisation are – to us surprisingly – subjected. The unfortunate aspect is that it is usually the American visitor who confuses accident and essence in this country. In this second half of the century, New Zealand finds itself moved by strategical considerations into the orbit of the United States, to whose strength so much was owed in the Pacific war. Despite outward appearances we have so much in common with the American people, and we covet their understanding no less than their goodwill in our alliance. We with them are part of the New World, though the New Zealander himself is different from the practical-minded Canadian, the volatile Australian, the stubborn South African and the uninhibited American.

Has New Zealand a characteristic contribution to make in the newer alignments of the western and southern hemispheres? To the world's troubled questions as to the survival of democracy, New Zealand has found an answer from its own experience and essential character.

While the free society can be defended by war it cannot be vindicated thereby. Technology may give the paramount nations the lead in nuclear fission or inter-stellar exploration, but it will of itself do no more for them in gaining the leadership of civilised man than the discovery of gunpowder did for the Chinese. Material achievements will not long satisfy - far less dominate - a world most in need of new ideas and ideals of social organisation.

The answer to confusion is never found in escape or in force. It lies in positive, peaceful achievement, and it is here that the conflict between democracy and communism must be resolved – if at all. It is precisely in this, in the comparative results of these rival forms of society, that democracy in New Zealand is meaningful.

It is an ancient principle that after the earthquake and the fire, wisdom may be found in the still small voice. It is in no mood of spiritual arrogance that small nations ask to be heard. It has been their role from the time of Socrates to voice the protest of conscience under the moral law.

New Zealand has learned that the pursuit of equality is not enough. The mechanics of a free society are not enough. Devotion to a beloved land is not enough. The readiness to defend human rights everywhere is not enough. These things we have and hold. But that which began in the hills of Judea with the concept of one God and of the law, still eludes the best we have achieved.

New Zealand believes that its continuing contribution must be in demonstrating that a people can come to full stature in a form of society wherein 'though there be armour and weapons, there is no need to display them' – because social and economic justice prevail.

6

LET THEM ENJOY THEIR FOOD, BEAUTIFY THEIR CLOTHING, BE

SATISFIED WITH THEIR HOMES, DELIGHT IN THEIR CUSTOMS

DISRAELI ONCE said that there's no egotism like that of a landed proprietor on a Sunday. It must be this feeling that overtakes a New Zealander surveying all that is his in this Small Utopia where, as Laotse anticipated, there is satisfaction, enjoyment and delight for all. Our Welfare Society has been described as the most advanced prototype in the world, yet New Zealanders are aware that the millenium is unaccountably delayed.

Those whose personal activities are restricted or whose individual wealth is reduced by the central regulation of the Welfare State are wont to say that New Zealand has gone too far and too fast; that to mitigate the element of hardness in human affairs is one thing, but to eliminate it is another thing altogether. The economist and the social scientist are likely to agree that the atmosphere of a Welfare Society is enervating where it particularly needs to be energising, and that the burden of contributory taxation is self-limiting. That most New Zealanders have voted for the immediate advantages of it all does not answer objections based upon more ultimate considerations.

What then are the broad facts?

New Zealand spends nearly half of its annual Budget on social services: 44 per cent as against 33.8 per cent in the USSR and 28.3 per cent in the United Kingdom. Within this total expenditure it costs the country 12 per cent of the Budget to maintain the health services. Almost a quarter of the Budget is spent on pensions, $2\frac{1}{2}$ times the proportion in the United Kingdom and more than $1\frac{1}{2}$ times that in the USSR.

Social services of this magnitude require one of the highest rates of taxation in the world. Expressed as a percentage of total income, the tax rate is exceeded only by that of West Germany and the

Netherlands, where entirely different objectives govern State expenditure.

This kind of wholesale disbursement can be evaluated only by what it buys, and it is here that the most cogent criticism of our social security system arises. As the distinguished President of the British Medical Association has pointed out, we are paying much more for a health service which is less complete than that of either the United Kingdom or Soviet Russia, though it is to be doubted whether in the latter, such services are as universally available as they are in New Zealand. He concludes his statistical survey of the various national systems by saying that when all allowances are made for the notorious difficulty of making useful comparisons on such a basis, it is not easy to escape the conviction that the people of New Zealand are paying too much for their State medical services. He recommends early rationalisation 'of the many provisions embarked upon in too easy-going and uncritical a fashion'.

In income tax and death duties, New Zealand wins first place. This undoubtedly serves the calculated purpose of redistributing national resources, but if this is in fact destroying incentive, then it incurs the law of diminishing returns. In England a lighthearted authority has argued that when national taxes pass 10 per cent of income, people begin to take evasive action; at 25 per cent, inflation debases the currency; and at more than 35 per cent, a nation is 'carting itself to history's junkpile'. It has very recently been estimated that taxes in New Zealand amount to 31.5 per cent of the national income. There may be a moral in this somewhere.

There are disquieting aspects of the national mentality. All human experience demonstrates that one cannot eat one's cake and still have it; but it is a feat that New Zealanders evidently hope to achieve with their national cake. They seem to expect government to perform with it a perpetual miracle of the loaves and fishes. As though 'free' State provisions do not have to be paid for, they demand more pay without increased output, better public amenities without increased rates, greater individual freedom to do as they desire in a society that takes a form which can only be run by bureaucracy. Despite the systematic sharing of wealth by graduated taxation, the chief New Zealand obsession is the pursuit of unearned increment from betting on horse races. By public demand, basic wages are pegged to the cost-of-living index rather than to any rate of production, so that many things cost more than they should, and those that are cheap are so usually because of State subsidies. This is of course rigging the market, however it may be justified on social grounds.

These are the familiar whipping boys in the New Zealand scene and of course they are not confined to this country. It is true that continued

36

prosperity would be more assured if New Zealanders set out to produce more, to design better, to sell abroad more aggressively, and to clear away restrictive practices in both management and the unions. But we seem to have read these precise criticisms of other nations, and with perhaps more force when the per capita production of New Zealand is the criterion. New Zealand's problems lie deeper than stock strictures on human nature.

The chief danger we face in this country lies in assuming – as too many of us do – that welfare provisions can exceed the net residue of national productivity. Rather must New Zealanders more generally understand what their politicians know all too well – that the balance between individual effort and political intervention requires a delicate and continuous adjustment. Clearly, it must be conceded that too many of us act as though prosperity is something you vote for.

We have been repeatedly warned that the special skills we need for our continued expansion can flourish only in an improved cultural climate, and that as a people we are too easily contented with the mediocre and the commonplace. Right attitudes towards skill would lead us to educate more for it and then give it due respect, status and reward; whether in higher margins for superior craftsmanship and performance, or in self-respecting salaries for our scientists, technologists, designers and creative writers.

New Zealand does need a new attitude toward the intellectual – he who creates, disseminates and applies culture. Over the whole nation they have been generally underpaid, unappreciated and all too often unheeded; and in turn they have tended to become recessive or hostile, indifferent or derisive toward the community that so little values them. This sense of alienation is undoubtedly one of the impoverishments of mental life in New Zealand, and it is said that we have neither the maturity nor the good sense to profit by the critical approach of our best minds. In the old taunting question: if we're so rich why aren't we smart?

Our typical work standards are said to be so dogged by the 'near enough's good enough' attitude as to be unsatisfactory to the markets we seek to win abroad; and that where our standards of design and finish are good, our costs and prices are not competitive. It follows, if this be true, that as more and more industries emerge into overseas competition they will seek to operate behind protective devices rather than within the economic price. The point to be grasped is that New Zealand is already competing abroad with success, and since there can be no special set of rules for emerging industry in this country we must fall into step with industrial efficiency everywhere. But defend ourselves as we will it still remains a fair question whether our future seems secure largely because it is as yet unexamined by the many who must make it.

Others have said that a community which claims to be so democratically free from class distinction makes itself look foolish by the exaggerated respect it accords the more ostentatious status-symbols of money. Our religious tolerance impresses some as being mere indifference; our racial tolerance as but the paternalism of an unthreatened majority. Our puritanism is the despair of visitors, reflected as it is in periodic referendums on the sale of alcoholic beverages, from which John Barley-corn always gets up again to sore surprise nobody. Yet our illogical liquor laws remain – neither one thing nor the other.

We like to think that in this half-acre of the world a sign has been given, and that anybody who understands it finds it promising. But some have found that the gospel according to New Zealand is just aggressively, complacently, self-righteously dull. They even hint that we are selective with the evidence.

We say that it has been our strength to be free from the doctrinaire; that we are a practical people concerned with compromise solutions of immediate problems, not theorists confined within a dogma. We claim that equality of opportunity and State security for all have proved to be a good working formula over a half-century of unparalleled stresses. Nevertheless our own economists, educators and social scientists are tugging at our sleeves and saying that this is all very well in practice, but how does it work out in principle. What will guide the generations that have known neither wars nor slumps; has natural law been suspended in our case so that greatness is no longer the child of adversity? It is fair to ask how long the Welfare Society can flourish on a declining moral imperative.

The investor, the industrialist, the worker – even the farmer – are coming to regard material security as synonymous with the good life; so that we ourselves are confusing means with ends. We have done well in subordinating private advantage to public interest; in insisting that the welfare of the common man must have the ultimate ascendancy in political considerations. But this is a day when every country is adding up its costs and starting to balance its books. Nor is this a matter for Government Audit. It is for every citizen to be his own assessor.

We believe that we have an answer to the critics of our Small Utopia. It is less than 150 years since the first furrow was driven by plough through New Zealand soil; only 122 years since formal Government was set up; only 100 years since the population of this country was three-quarters of a million people, without a single railway, telegraph, electric light, freezing works, or university; less than 90 years since central government began to unify the country; less than 20 years since New Zealand assumed formal national independence within the British Commonwealth of Nations.

New Zealand has made a good start. It has had time for little more than that. Ahead of us lies continuing endeavour in these islands of achievement, for islands of achievement they certainly are.

A survey of the welfare society turns out to be a survey of the economic possibilities for mankind. It shows what progress this small country has made during twenty-odd years of basic investment in human capital. Its most momentous conclusion is that full social welfare sustains itself by the steady development it fosters.

Despite all the lugubrious talk of disincentives, of the self-limitation of extravagant demands on current production, of discouragement of investment funds and capital resources, the welfare society in New Zealand has proved itself to be workable, profitable and continuable within the overall economic price.

Value judgments against it will no doubt continue to be made by those who prefer individual advantage to corporate progress, prejudice being what it is – vagrant opinion without visible means of support. Others with more acceptable motives may still fear that the case is yet unproven and that to share the cake more evenly conspires against a larger cake. Whatever the textbooks may say, it has been demonstrated in New Zealand that the disincentive of taxation is compensated by the added incentive of larger and steadier market demand.

Admittedly, the care of the aged is costly. It accounts for nearly a quarter of this country's welfare expenditure. On humanitarian grounds we refuse to abandon these, our own people, and on economic grounds the proper thing to do turns out to be the best thing to do. We have certainly learned that it is economically advantageous to distribute purchasing power through pensions no less than through wages. The progressive elimination of means tests is proving that point.

The vindication of welfare principles in New Zealand has thus become a private enterprise as much as a socialist doctrine. It emerges from the rapidity and healthiness of the economic development it promotes; a development which is now seen to be a cause rather than an effect of prosperity. Therefore it is not the 'ism' under which such development is achieved that is important any more, but the increasing acceptance of welfare principles by all parties of political integrity.

This has been New Zealand's best contribution to social and political economy.

7

NEEDING NEVER TO MOVE OUTSIDE THEIR OWN

COUNTRY

THE CULTURAL life of New Zealand has seemed to some observers to be as insubstantial as Macbeth's witches – as well it might when one looks in the wrong place for the wrong thing at the wrong time.

It is obvious enough that the practical urgencies of pioneer life in any country can give little encouragement to literature and the fine arts. Yet from the beginning there were in New Zealand men and women of sensibility who recorded their interpretations of this new land in narrative, social reflection, satire, humour, and even poetry, of some distinction; and the early work in the visual arts had many chaste examples of the period at its best.

So long as these authors and artists had their roots in the old world which continued to dominate their outlook, and until the turn of the century when native-born New Zealanders began to outnumber expatriated Britons, a New Zealand tradition could scarcely emerge. Indeed, some of the earlier intellectuals found the general inelegance of mind quite insupportable, and migrated in search of a spiritual home in the northern hemisphere.

As G. B. Shaw pointed out during his visit in 1934, any man who follows his profession is more or less bound to follow his market. New Zealand is no literary centre as are America and London and Paris, which must continue to attract our best minds. But where it was once felt that to be a New Zealander is to be an exile, it is no longer true that intellectual satisfaction and emotional sensitivity can only be found elsewhere. We are becoming aware of ourselves as an individual society, so that nowadays our authors and artists are illuminating the human situation with mastery, insight and imagination. That is surely the mark of maturity – to know the best that has been thought, said and done by mankind,and to find one's native inheritance a challenge and a stimulus.

The corrosive spirit of the thirties and the disenchantment of the war years produced what was perhaps the first truly indigenous writing in New Zealand; literature of protest for the most part, with here and there the language of hope as well as of despair. Of recent years our novelists have won recognition in world company with book-society best-sellers that have attracted even the film-makers' dubious patronage. One of our leading poets has received the accolade of publication by the Oxford University Press, and our historians, educators and anthropologists have an international reputation. It is demonstrably untrue that remoteness imposes only impoverishment of mind and spirit.

This development may be traced in the visual arts as well. At first, our painters sought to make credible the visible beauties of the New Zealand landscape and its luminous atmosphere, in water colour, oil paintings and drawings of considerable technical skill. The visitor will be repaid for an hour or two in any of our early colonist art galleries, where may be seen some quite remarkable work, even to modern eyes. Some of these artists were topographers and surveyors who not unnaturally depicted with the stylised precision of the draughtsman all the variety of our towering, bush-clad mountains, the set-pieces of tumbling rivers and the brave new world a-building on the plains. They too saw it as a new England or Scotland – unencumbered and inviting the transplantation of the familiar and the beloved of the old world. As successive waves of settlers arrived, they brought with them the furniture, pictures and books; the designs for houses, churches and council-chambers; the trees, hawthorn hedges and gorse; the farm implements, clothing fashions and needlecraft that represented the culture of their homeland. For long enough it understandably occupied the artist and the artisan alike.

The avenues of oaks and planes, poplars and cypress still remind us of our origins; ghost towns can still be found asleep with their memories of gold-mining days; village smithies of pit-hewn timber lie here and there, leaning derelict against their neighbours, cluttered with the iron, wood and leather-ware of the horse era. We have acquired a past, something aged of our own; so the artist of today is learning to express by impressionism what the representation of nature never could. There is growing an inner significance as well as an outward beauty in this country.

New Zealand today has a high proportion of significant inter-preters whose work is sought by the discerning. Our leading artists, wood-engravers and etchers hold their place in international com-pany; our concert pianists and violinists perform and record as international virtuosi; we produce prima ballerinas and principal danseurs. That there is a sense of adventure and perceptiveness in public attitudes toward the arts is evident in the large numbers who attend exhibitions from overseas which make no concessions to easy understanding.

The arts of ballet and music are likely to be least lively in isolation yet the New Zealand Ballet Company, the New Zealand Opera Company and the National Symphony Orchestra are comparable with provincial companies abroad, on the testimony of the distinguished foreign directors and conductors they attract from time to time.

Professional soloists, chamber-musicians and famous-name orchestras such as the Boston Symphony and the Czech Philharmonic find it rewarding to come to this country, and for their performances thousands of our people travel as far as four hundred miles for seats at prices that are inevitably expensive. Here again, visiting artists are generous to a degree in their tributes to the enthusiasm and perception of New Zealand audiences.

Professional drama holds a somewhat precarious place in so small a population, but there are more than thirty thousand New Zealanders actively engaged in the amateur dramatic movement, a proportion of one in eighty of the population. The production of as many as thirty full-length plays in the season is not uncommon in any of our main cities, their general competence and occasional excellence by any standards, demonstrating the vigour with which drama flourishes here. The New Zealand Drama Council, the Community Arts Service and the Adult Education Service foster one-act festivals which bring together each year thousands of participants. Though only a minority of our people attend the theatre, we are led to believe that the proportion is higher than in England or America. Few theatre-goers are unaware of the works of Anouilh, Beckett, Ugo Betti and Berthold Brecht. More significantly, our own writers are producing workmanlike plays which are published overseas and widely performed in New Zealand. The flourishing record industry of the country is now presenting our own artists in classical and popular entertainment which constitutes an increasing proportion of broadcast fare; the practice and appreciation of art is in the curriculum of almost every secondary school in New Zealand, and school orchestras' performances are as athletic as their schoolmasters' conducting. There are two University Schools of Art and upwards of twenty Art Societies, at least one-third of whose members exhibit in the annual Shows. Governmental grants to cultural activities in the form of subsidies to societies and bursaries for gifted students, together with grants for literary publication, increase substantially year by year. Literary periodicals, books of verse, choral societies, festivals of music, speech and drama, pipe band and brass band competitions of the highest order, more than fifty Film Society groups and a National Film Studio whose work regularly wins foreign awards – all this cultural activity adds up to a national accomplishment by no means contemptible.

Yet the impression is abroad that aided by our wonderful outdoor climate and a rude isolation from the world's major intellectual currents, New Zealanders live like a colony of profane yogis, assiduously mortifying the spirit for the good life of the flesh!

Comparison of the cultural life of any sizeable New Zealand city with its counterpart in other countries will hardly be to our disadvantage. The culture of the world's great centres – London, Paris, New York, Moscow – does not represent the common levels of taste, perception and sensitivity of their own populations, and even less those of the English, French, American and Russian nations. The cultural ascendancy of older societies inheres in their elite few and in the narrowest definition of culture.

Elite groups emerge from three sources; birth, property, and personal achievement. For a variety of reasons, New Zealand has chosen an economic and social pattern which favours only the third. Founded with an aversion to any aristocracy of blood, this country has more recently equalised the power of property and wealth by redistributive policies that have opened the way for an elite based upon personal achievement. The prejudiced are pleased to predict that in a classless society this principle will fail for lack of incentive. That remains a moot question. We have certainly not proved that all men and women are equally educable, that aspiration automatically follows opportunity or that fine arts are equally fine for all. What has been done to a marked degree is to provide the means to the good life so that where it is not being pursued as it could be, this is through the unconstrained choice of the individual and not because of some imposed social or economic disability. New Zealanders would consider this to be propitious for their cultural growth.

The truly interesting thing being tested in this country is whether this faith in the common man, in his ability to improve himself and his lot, and in his natural response to opportunity, will be justified by uncommon achievement. The elevation of a whole people is a protracted undertaking, lacking the spectacular accomplishments associated with technological objectives.

In this country the human situation is paramount. The ancient world erected its culture upon helotry, the mediaeval upon serfdom, the modern upon money-power. In this age and particularly in this country the aristocratic tradition is irrelevant. We are our own masters

44

in very real and direct terms; we have our own objectives, and by them alone should we be judged.

The aristocratic tradition holds that culture and egalitarianism are incompatible: to mix them is to end up with muddled mediocrity. Mediocrity can certainly be found in New Zealand, for there are large numbers of prejudiced and ignorant people in every nation, and many who are too easily satisfied. Unfortunately that is all some people see wherever they go, and those with a point to make, having found it, look no further. By the authority of repetition, this rubric of New Zealand's general witlessness has been accepted by the odd Fulbrighter, the patronising journalist and the traveller inconsolable without a private bathroom. Mediocrity awaits these people every-where.

There is a time-scale of culture. Greek society, for example, did not begin with the Parthenon: it began with a shepherd's hut and a goatherd's pipe on a hillside; there were wood-carvers before there were masons and sculptors, politicians and priests before there were poets, dramatists and philosophers. Moreover it all required half a millenium for its fulfilment. A hundred and twenty years is little enough time in which to build an advanced social order based upon democratic humanism. If New Zealand has not matched the temples, statues and free-ranging thought of ancient Greece, the art master-pieces and palaces of the Renaissance, or the skyscraper opulence of today, it has to its credit other achievements which may be contributing something of value to the democratic culture of the future.

* * * *

In the hands of the many rather than the few, the character-istically amateur culture of this country emerges as a composite of the housewife's domestic management no less than the special skills of the artist, poet, musician and playwright. It is compounded of all the activities and leisure interests of the whole people: the furniture, boats, radio-sets, go-karts and gliders that they build in home work-shops; regatta day, rugby football, horse racing and the A. and P. Show. It ranges from the market town with its sale-day conviviality and its rural carnival of woodchopping, sheep-dog trials and wool-shearing, to the city with its fashion-parades, continental eating-houses, action-painting, junk-sculpture, abstractionism and bohem-ian poets. It embraces the diversity of neo-Gothic universities, lamb and mint sauce, the music of custom-built hi-fi rigs, blossom festivals, potteries, mountaineering, food-and-wine societies and unarmed police. It includes all the intellectual errors and emotional prejudices reflected in our sensitiveness to any sort of criticism; the peculiarities of our language, loyalties and customs.

Is all this a tenable definition of culture, or must it be confined within the conventional notion of finesse in the fine arts? Is this muddled mixture merely democracy on the brain?

Such a broad definition can find historic roots in the Middle Ages, when culture was similarly integral with everyday life. Their architects were foremen builders, their sculptors were masons, their illuminators and artists were clerks. They did not talk of "fine arts", though they had them. They just built cathedrals, candlesticks, chessmen, cheese-presses and sculptures as part of the business of living and providing. In much the same fashion the ancient Greeks also held this attitude toward culture as part of common life in its fullness. They did not classify it as a thing apart and for adepts only. Indeed, they had no word for it. Their sculptors did not even bother to sign their work, nor would it have occurred to them that they possessed some separate commodity which was the product of an aloof elite, something that could be admired and emulated as an end in itself. What we call Greek culture emerged by the simple process of common aspiration, by the gradual refinement of everyday things, by the elaboration of language, and the cultivation of all that they did together as a people.

There is therefore precedent for defining culture as the organised outcome of community experience, including all that a people makes and does; its material goods and possessions, its institutions and services; all that it has elaborated in attitudes and beliefs, ideas and judgments; its social and political organisation as well as its arts and sciences. Only this sort of conspectus can reflect the real character of a people.

New Zealand seems to have proceeded on the belief that the fine arts would develop as the people lived usefully and progressively; and that the aesthetic sense, far from being the endowment of the fine-born, fine-drawn few, is inherent in the many and merely awaits an encouraging environment. Has the event justified this faith?

The spread of the aesthetic sense is uneven. The remoter back-blocks are scarcely the place to exhibit Henry Moore, nor can it be pretended that the hosts in the cities who attend public exhibitions of such sculpture all remain to pray. For the New Zealander culture is not something to be taken up in a humourless haze of high-seriousness. The people read widely enough to be aware of the hoax that constitutes so much of "modern" art, and there is no class of patrons for whom the outrageous is an approved status symbol with nothing to recommend it but the price-tag. The artistic adventurer in this small country is restrained within the solace of his own satisfaction. There are few pecuniary inducements to eccentricity. We are therefore spared the worst follies of the masquerade and our silly seasons are mercifully short. We have for most of the time other things to do, and general public interest is more likely to be aroused in the fitness of design in a national gift to a royal princess, the architectural lay-out of school buildings, the purchases for art galleries or the style of speech adopted by broadcasters. Such periodic controversies disclose a surprising awareness of the difference between design and decoration, significant form and insignificant shape, cult and culture. Letters to the editor cannot be ignored in any evaluation of the New Zealanders' state of mind.

Because the family unit has always been the chief custodian and the best conduit of a people's culture – as distinct from that of an elite – New Zealand family life must also be examined. It is doubtful whether a man ever escapes his heritage, biological or environmental. Consequently, the family is an institution of which nearly everybody speaks well. New Zealand regards it as something by which we should also do well. Nor are we as a people content that the housewife and mother no longer copes at subsistence level. The whole bias of life in this country is toward the point where according to her good sense she is able to give her family the scale of familial values and virtues which represents the best that she knows. It is the limitation of life to know better than we do. New Zealand homes are good, bad and indifferent; but none need be determined by anything other than the family itself, certainly not by the denial of fundamental human rights. It is at this level that our welfare society operates most purposefully.

Our representative family lives in its own home, replete with mortgage; which will be under controlled terms, particularly if it be held by the State Advances Corporation. The house will be detached, standing in its own lawns and gardens, for even in our largest cities we are not largely tenement dwellers. It will have the labour-saving devices, probably a motorcar, a musical instrument for the two or three children, and several radio-sets, one of which will be a radio-gramophone. New Zealand has been one of the best per capita markets for classical records, and the statistics support the view that this medium has played a major role in making our people musically discerning. There will be rather too much furniture; ornaments that vary from the mass-produced to pieces of the finest English porcelain; an assortment of books, a stamp collection, women's magazines, in the children's rooms the paraphernalia of sport, and everywhere an air of wellbeing and easy, informal hospitality. Neighbourliness is strongly developed in the typical New Zealand community.

Any of these homes, suburban or rural, is likely to reflect a wide range of human interest and activities – mechanical, social and

47

cultural. For one thing, there is the everlasting tinkering with that mechanical slave of a green-grass country, the motormower, whose whine is the universal accompaniment of the weekend at home. Another mechanical preoccupation is the care and maintenance of the motorcar, which may vary from the vintage and the veteran to the hot-rod. In a country where automobile prices are amongst the highest in the world, New Zealanders contrive to keep their cars going in a tenacity of life that would astonish their makers. Then there is the housepainting and interior redecoration of a race of inveterate do-it-yourselfers. In this country nobody lives further than 80 miles from the sea, and over three-quarters of our people live within a half-hour's drive of it, to say nothing of the innumerable lakes and rivers. So weekend summer leisure is spent largely by the water, where so many families have built their own bach or crib – the name varies from north to south – and where swimming, surf-casting, ocean fishing or small-boat sailing are everybody's business.

The social life of the family will be built round the group organisation which is unique in New Zealand. Sports bodies are legion, from the primary schools' competitions through to the universities' tournaments; from local, district, provincial and national associations of football, athletics, swimming and basketball, to Empire Games and Olympic Games selection. In the country, horse events attain world standards; in the cities highly organised sports meetings vary from night-trotting and stockcar racing to aquatic carnivals, winter shows, outdoor wrestling and boxing, and aero-club pageants. At the heart of it all, the family unit organises itself according to its tastes. The mother will be a good cook and a zealous baker of cakes for the local church bazaar and the PTA; she will be houseproud and perhaps a trifle oppressive in her insistence on the family's use of the doormat and the butterknife. The father is likely to be a homebrewer of passable beer, a member of a golf, bowling, cricket or football club – according to the age of his arteries – as an escape hatch from the prevailing domesticity. The man's world of sport is important to a New Zealander all the days of his life. New Zealanders are a green-fingered people with special skills in flower and vegetable gardens. Ours is a climate where most things can be grown out of doors and nurserymen supply almost everything under the sun. The youngsters will probably belong to the Scouts or Guides; will not be over-given to restraint in speech or manners, and they will certainly see more of apples than of the doctor. The whole family will holiday together in motor-camp, caravan or tent till the teen-agers hive off for tramping, climbing or ski-sports.

This is a fair picture of representative family life in New Zealand. It provokes its share of anxious scrutiny by parents and social workers

48

where it deviates from this healthy and agreeable pattern, but despite its quota of juvenile delinquency, the New Zealand family is stable and conservative in habit, well-served by governmental provisions; from family-benefit allowances, through school, medical and health services to home-building programmes. Its ties are enduring, and its care of its aged tends to make common the three-generation unit, bonded in loyalty and affection. This is true not of the few only, but of the majority of our families.

*   *   *   *

The next most formative influence in a people's culture is its schools. Standards of home-conduct and school-attainment have always been so inter-related that it is no new thing to have the two institutions reproaching each other for failures in either. Without close relationship, it is fatally easy for them to weave as did Penelope awaiting Ulysses – the work done by day, unravelled at night. Awareness of this crucial relationship is evident in the Home and School Association, a name that is replacing the earlier Parent-Teacher Association title. Some observers have expressed surprise at what seems to them to be a too-authoritarian discipline in New Zealand schools and a too-lax control at home. This view tends to be cancelled out by other criticisms which simply reverse the charges. To some it is odd to find a people so decidedly individual and independent in their family life, entrusting to the schools so much in the areas of training in moral conduct, character development, personal hygiene, sex instruction and even religion. It is easy to forget how past generations lacked the basic biological knowledge and were too inhibited by the Victorian tradition to handle certain of these matters in either home or school. It was inevitable that progressive education should undertake training for social adaptability and full citizenship, and natural that the school should increasingly become an extension of the home. It has long been an educational ideal that the school should be a bridge between familial protection and individual independence.

New Zealand sees democracy in education as based upon the belief that each person is entitled to the educational opportunities and individual instruction best suited to his full potential as a person and a citizen. These are brave words, as old as Athens. By its commitment to this ideal, New Zealand now finds itself in the eye of the storm; pledged to universal education of this content for an exploding school population. In 1939 the total university enrolment was under 6,000: by 1972 it is projected at 30,000 – a five-fold increase in a third of a century. At secondary levels the country is now experiencing the impact of the "post-war babies" generation; yet by 1972 the third-form enrolments will be up fifty per cent on present swollen figures. The primary schools are crowded by the same pressure of our high birth-rate. That is the quantitative problem.

As the general educational level rises, and our expectations for each next generation rise accordingly, what steps must be taken to meet the educational capacity which has also been rising steadily? What the outstanding few alone could do yesterday, the many average students will be able to do tomorrow: can democratic education keep ahead of democratic needs? There is the qualitative problem.

The trouble with making education a sort of secular religion, as we have tended to do in New Zealand, is not so much that it leads us to expect too much of our schools as that it leads us to expect the wrong things. Our school system, for instance, has little power to inculcate a greater respect for standards of performance, for learning, taste, intelligence and excellence than the community as a whole really feels. We but delude ourselves if we expect the educational system to maintain ideals of achievement that the community as a whole has abandoned or never held. The need for people of superior imagination, training and drive is much greater than we can supply, but New Zealand too often gives the impression that we have been so persuaded that all God's chillun must have shoes, that we think they've all got the same-sized feet.

In this country an educated society is accomplished fact, but we have yet to capitalise the exceptional student. On the one hand we expect the schools to teach our children by intellectual and moral discipline how to think, to observe and to evaluate the society they inherit; and on the other hand we require the delivery of vocational skills for an economy gravely undersupplied in almost every area of performance. There is nothing wrong about such demands since both are the accepted task of modern education. What is unrealistic is to expect the education of all – even the dullards – to superior standards in parallel with specialised training for the exceptional individual in the face of an acute and chronic teacher shortage at all levels.

For all their innovation, modernity, freedom and widening functions, New Zealand schools cannot escape the built-in limitations of democratic education. A highway open to all and without tolls is likely to be over-crowded, unruly, its pace unaccommodating to faster traffic, its control complicated and any changes of direction hazardous. With a school population roughly doubling every decade, and the future wholly dependent upon the quality of their education, we should realise that if there are experts in the wisdom of life they cannot be mass-produced or supplied to order in even the most determined democracy. Perhaps we do. Perhaps the annually increased education vote will take care of everything. The current reappraisal

50

of the education system has been energising as well as agonising and we seem to realise that we get no more than we pay for. If a child's education should begin at least a hundred years before it is born, perhaps somebody else is to blame for our deficiencies. It is probably true to say that New Zealand is better prepared for the verdict of a hundred years hence than most countries of the world. It is as a cultural force that our schools must look ahead.

*   *   *   *

Yet another repository of a people's standards, codes and ethics are the learned professions and the skilled trades. In its professional traditions, New Zealand has followed the cultural pattern of Britain. The medical profession, for example, has long looked to the United Kingdom for post-graduate training, though this is changing with the development of the Australasian Colleges of Physicians and of Surgeons, and the institution of postgraduate centres within New Zealand. As a result of this traditional reciprocity, New Zealand doctors occupy a high proportion of important Commonwealth posts, and have indeed made plastic surgery in Britain a virtual annexe of their specialism. Medical and hospital practice within this country is of a high order, a reflection of which is the selection in two successive years of a New Zealander as President of the parent British Medical Association.

Ever since Lord Rutherford of Nelson left his mark as probably the greatest experimental physicist since Newton, New Zealand has had its eminent representatives in overseas scientific research centres. The penetration of our engineers throughout the world has long been a matter of unamused comment in the countries of their adoption, where their eminence commands an altogether disproportionate number of the top jobs. New Zealand scholars are to be found in so many parts of the world as to warrant the conclusion that this country has found equalitarianism by no means incompatible with a strong academic culture.

In trade crafts we have developed certain specialised skills in both design and execution, of which the water-jet motor-boat is but one of the more recent evidences. The absence of major mass production by comparison with that of the great populations has fostered a marked capacity among our technical tradesmen for precision skills. Handicraft expertness is in fact a characteristic of New Zealand's manual culture, something that was amply demonstrated during the war in all theatres and wherever our maintenance units served ashore and afloat. This was particularly true of our aircraft, transport and radio technicians.

The things we make in New Zealand are not all a matter for exultation. Visitors have commented on our taste in domestic and hotel furniture. It is patchy indeed, dominated as it is by the economic factor. We do not seem to have an indigenous furniture designed in its own right and persisting by its intrinsic virtue as has the American colonial style. Nor do we have a great deal of valuable period furniture from England and Europe, so that our knowledge of it is more confined to reproductions than originals. But those with appreciation can testify to the fine craftsmen in most centres who can repair the original piece with the same devoted care with which they copy it. If this imitation be held against them, our craftsmen are well enough informed to remind us how little of England's cherished period furniture was actually made by the great designers — the Adam brothers, Hepplewhite or Sheraton – and how much was made "in the style" by nameless workers who were none the less skilful or their creations any the less valuable on that account.

There are distinctive churches and cathedrals throughout the country, built at successive stages of our architectural evolution; and when an adequate history of New Zealand architecture comes to be written, justice may be done to the designers and builders from Selwyn's finely adapted wooden Gothic down to the contemporary emphases that rebut the common charge that their work is merely repetitive. Nor are these churches centres of bigotry. New Zealanders are not a deeply spiritual people, but the social values of Christian protest are integral in our culture. It is said that our welfare system was conceived in broad pattern by three men – a minister of religion, a medical practitioner, and a journalist – who during the Depression years met regularly to talk out their indignation and their aspiration for the community. All three entered Parliament in order to change the situation, and one of them continues to play a dominant role in politics. That sort of direct action can happen in a small country: that kind of militant Christian action can succeed in a democracy. The sometimes criticised home-spun character of our Parliamentary representatives is a New Zealand trade-mark, a sign of our commonalty.

* * * *

The three instruments of cultural diffusion, literature, the press and radio broadcasting, can have but passing comment. The national appetite for reading has been referred to. It supports a great number of book stores which in the cities are modern, commodious and well stocked and which everywhere complain that import licencing restricts the variety of the better, and the volume of all, literature available to the public. To the extent that this is true it indicts official thinking and conspires against the fuller mental life which underpins all culture. There is nevertheless a wide range of books and periodicals from all parts of the English speaking world, and nobody can claim that in this country books fail of their job as the true levellers. Censorship of literature does exist, infrequently invoked, and then only to prevent our bookstores becoming nurseries of wantonness. Some day, someone in high quarters may read Voltaire's letter to the commissioner of Police of Paris and be advised that if there had been censorship of literature in Rome we should have today neither Horace nor Juvenal nor the philosophical writings of Cicero. Meantime, New Zealand publishing houses have respectable lists of fiction, biography, history, poetry, exploration, travel, mountaineering and every kind of sport. The visitor may be agreeably surprised at the range of our New Zealand authors published both abroad and at home.

Our press is lively and independent, moderate in tone (though in early days it was rich in invective and tireless in local logrolling) almost uniformly discreet in its reticences, and very much a watch dog of public interest. Of the forty-odd daily newspapers that collectively reach saturation point, none is a national organ capable of king-making. Circulation varies from a provincial thousand to a metropolitan two hundred thousand, almost all of it good journalism and all of it too-heavily weighted with advertising. As a guardian of public morality, political integrity and the approved domestic virtues our newspapers can be regarded as a cultural medium in good standing.

Radio broadcasting, as a State monopoly, tends to be timorous and conservative, but government control has at least kept the system free from the abuses of disc-jockey payola and bogus quizz-programmes which have plagued privately-owned networks elsewhere. The commercial stations with their advertising income support the losses incurred by the non-commercial stations, a despoiling of the philistines in favour of the muses which seems to be the most defensible subsidy of them all. Now we have television, long resisted and reluctantly surrendered to. Whether it will become a juke-box of foreign shoddy or a creditable institution will be a test of New Zealand's redoubtable capacity for compromise. Unless technological advances can cheapen programme costs, the former is the likely fate of all small countries venturing into what is essentially a mass-medium.

*   *   *   *

All this is a summary interpretation of New Zealand's cultural life. It began necessarily with the agriculture, animal husbandry, horticulture and silviculture which afford us food, clothing and shelter. It broadened into programmes of human welfare by universal education and social provision. It continues under an anxiously benevolent State system that is desirous of adding cubits to our every stature. Does it yet amount to anything more than a culture of pots and pans? Any answer that a New Zealander may give is subject to the charge of chauvinism. So it must be left to others to formulate their own judgment.

Where New Zealanders hold too rigid views as to what is relevant to our way of life we constrain our interests and perpetuate our prejudices. For cultural maturity we need more than the mechanics of democracy, and its dynamics will move us only as we cultivate excellence for its own sake and beyond the needs of livelihood and the cash nexus.

Matthew Arnold anticipated our form of society in which there would be no arbitrary limitations, and he proposed for it a charter:

> "What brings about a natural, rational life, satisfying to the modern spirit? This: the growth of a love of industry, trade and wealth; of the love of things of the mind; of the love of beautiful things. There are body, intelligence and soul taken care of."

New Zealand could well seek more of the "sweetness and light" which were for Matthew Arnold the core of all culture, individual and national. Observers who come fault-finding rather than fact-finding have an easy task. Ours is too controversial a society to escape critical analysis, and little will be found here of the glory that was Greece or the grandeur that is Rome. In the view section that follows we cannot hope to capture more than a fraction of the natural beauty which is beyond criticism. It is this above all that makes a visit to New Zealand memorable. It is in this at least that the observer may agree with Laotse: that for scenic beauty unadorned the New Zealander need never move outside his own country. As a matter of fact we do, in our hundreds of thousands. So we have a particularly warm feeling towards travellers who reciprocate our visits abroad. We covet for them the kindliness and hospitality which we ourselves have received and of which our fellow New Zealanders are so richly capable.

THE PHOTOGRAPHS

Once the New Zealand forest stretched heavy and moist and dark from snowline to the sea. Its evergreen foliage was so thick that it excluded light and air in a natural conservatory, in which flourished a flora unique in the world. Remote, unspoiled and sealed in silence, it still mantles much of the high country.

A former Governor-General, Lord Bledisloe, who, in England, was the Senior Verderer of the ancient Forest of Dean said, in opening New Plymouth's beautiful Brooklands Park: "New Zealand possesses many outstanding natural advantages, but in two respects it is unique; one is the number, variety and grandeur of its beauty spots; the other is its native bush without rival anywhere. I make bold to prophecy that New Zealand's main source of wealth will be found not in its sheep-breeding or dairy-farming but in its tourist traffic".

In 1934, this seemed a mere flight of fancy, especially to the audience of Taranaki farmers. But since then hundreds of thousands of tourists have proved Lord Bledisloe a true prophet. Only now are New Zealanders beginning to value their country's natural assets and to organise adequate facilities for tourist enjoyment. And one of the greatest joys the discerning visitor can find in New Zealand is the sight of the beauty of the bush free from the taint of commercial exploitation.

Overleaf
Left. The Gorge Falls, South Fiord, Lake Te Anau.
PHOTOGRAPH, NATIONAL PUBLICITY STUDIOS

Opposite
A giant Kauri tree, Waipoua Forest, Northland.
PHOTOGRAPH, STEELE PHOTOGRAPHY

Right. A fern-fringed track near Fox Glacier, Weheka, South Westland.
PHOTOGRAPH, NATIONAL PUBLICITY STUDIOS

The most remarkable of our native birds are the flightless forms; the notornis, long thought to be extinct but rediscovered in 1949 deep in the uninhabited snow-grass country of Fiordland; and the Kiwi, tailless, wingless, blind by day, with its nostrils at the tip instead of the base of its long bill. Elusive, a night feeder and eating its own weight in worms each day, the kiwi, with its acute sense of smell, detects the worm by its surface cast and seeks it deep in the ground with its long beak. The kiwi farm in Hawkes Bay has succeeded, where overseas zoo curators have failed, in breeding the bird in captivity.

Imported stoats, weasels and cats have reduced the bird population; but the lovely notes of the bellbird and the liquid burble of the tui may still be heard in the quiet places where these delicate honey-eaters plunder the nectar of the kowhai and flowering gum. The native pigeon, once snared with guile by the ancient Maori for its delectable flesh, is now a protected citizen. Everywhere will be seen the inquisitive fantail that seems to love human company but really comes indoors to seek flies. The mournful night cry of the "morepork" can be heard in most country places, the native owl whose sound was so often imitated by the Maori warrior as his pre-dawn signal for an attack on redoubt or encampment.

Our native seabirds include the terns, gannets and gulls that drift along the coast, bleakly wailing a storm warning as they come inland for shelter. In the marshy lakelands live the long billed long legged waders – the stilt, swamphen and godwit – whilst in the far south the penguins remind us that 1,600 miles below the horizon lies Antarctica, for whose exploration New Zealand is the base of many international operations.

As Australia has its platypus, New Zealand has its famed 'living fossil' the tuatara lizard, sole survivor of a species extinct elsewhere for millions of years. These strange creatures may be seen in the zoos of Auckland and Wellington but their only natural habitat is the Hen and Chicken Islands, near the entrance to Whangarei harbour.

Opposite
Top. The Kiwi, one of New Zealand's national emblems.
PHOTOGRAPH, NATIONAL PUBLICITY STUDIOS

Bottom. The Tuatara Lizard.
PHOTOGRAPH, STEELE PHOTOGRAPHY

In the far north of Northland are the gum fields where, in the days before synthetics, a thriving industry supplied the amber-like, petrified secretion of Kauri trees to the world's varnish manufacturers. Today there is almost no market for natural gum, but a few old-timers still retain their diggings, waiting for the rise in prices that, they hope, will return their hoard to its former value.

On the west coast lies Ninety Mile beach. From this enormous sweep of smooth, hard sand, Kingsford Smith took off in his Fokker monoplane, "Southern Cross", on March 26th, 1933, on the return journey to Mascot Aerodrome, Sydney, after his second trans-Tasman flight, and again for his homeward journey on his sixth flight in April, 1934, and C.T.P. Ulm departed in his Avro monoplane, "Faith in Australia" in April, 1934. In the pioneering days of aviation, landing fields for lumbering, overladen aircraft were few and far between, but New Zealand's very distance, beyond stormy seas was a challenge to every would-be record-breaker in the British Commonwealth. Not all of them found land, or saw beneath them this first inviting glimpse of New Zealand; but nowadays the beach is a familiar sight to Pacific and Tasman air travellers speeding to the country's international airports.

The Bay of Islands is the base for some of the world's finest and most beautiful fishing grounds and is itself one of the most historic places in New Zealand. At the Bay of Islands, the first New Zealand colonists landed in 1826, and it was here, at Waitangi, that the famous treaty with the Maori people was signed in 1840.

The West Coast road south from the Bay of Islands runs through the Waipoua forest, the last remaining vestige of kauri forest that retains its virgin character in any marked degree. Several of the giant kauri trees are easily accessible from the highway; this memorable drive through dense native rain forest is one of the most striking in the country.

Whangarei, capital of Northland, lies snugly about the headwaters of Whangarei harbour, looking out upon the Pacific Ocean. This bustling, rapidly expanding Borough of some 22,000 people is the commercial centre for a thriving farming district.

Looking north along Ninety Mile Beach from Tauroa Point.

PHOTOGRAPH, NATIONAL PUBLICITY STUDIOS

The Treaty House, Waitangi, overlooks the scene of New Zealand's earliest history. Some distance away, on a spot visible across the water, the pioneer Anglican missionary Rev. Samuel Marsden preached the first Christian sermon to the Maori people, on Christmas Day, 1814. A couple of hundred yards in front of the Treaty House the flagstaff marks the spot where in February 1840 the first Lieutenant-Governor, Captain William Hobson R.N. negotiated the Treaty of Waitangi which united the two races under the formal rule of the British Crown.

During their term of office, Their Excellencies Lord and Lady Bledisloe purchased this historic site, created it the Waitangi National Trust and gifted the property of over a thousand acres with the old British Residency to the nation as a memorial. In the muniment rooms are many relics of bygone days, and in the whare runanga a magnificent collection of specimens of Maori art.

This is the cradle of New Zealand's constitutional history, fittingly set in the unrivalled beauty of the Bay of Islands.

The Treaty House, Waitangi, Bay of Islands.
PHOTOGRAPH, NATIONAL PUBLICITY STUDIOS

Between 1861 and 1961, the population of urban Auckland had grown from 10,000 to 450,000, making it by far the largest city in New Zealand in both population and area. With freedom to expand upon flat land to north and south, it has become one of the most dispersed cities in the world. Aucklanders therefore insist that Captain William Hobson, first Lieutenant Governor of the new colony, was absolutely right in choosing this site as the capital of New Zealand, and that only a wicked conspiracy removed the seat of Government to Wellington in 1865.

It had been a remarkable bargain in 1840; an area of about 3,000 acres bought from the Maoris for "£55 in money, 50 blankets, 20 trousers, 20 sheets, 10 caps, 4 casks of tobacco, 1 box of pipes, 1000 yards of gown pieces, 10 iron pots, 1 bag of sugar, 1 bag of flour and 20 hatchets". Today the Auckland City Council controls 8,697 acres with a capital ratable value close to £176,000,000.

Auckland has been likened to Rome with its seven hills, to Corinth in its isthmus setting and to Naples in its harbour aspect. Aucklanders prefer Lord Northcliffe's unequivocal opinion: "the most beautifully situated city in the world". Containing 18 per cent of the country's total population, Auckland is also the greatest commercial and manufacturing centre and the leading port of the country.

Two institutions particularly merit the attention of visitors – the Public Library and Art Gallery situated in the heart of the city, and the War Memorial Museum on its magnificent site in the Public Domain a mile away but overlooking the city centre. The Polynesian exhibits of the War Memorial Museum are among the finest in the world.

View across Auckland City Centre from the Waitemata Harbour (on the Pacific) in the foreground, to the Manakau Harbour (on the Tasman) in the background.

PHOTOGRAPH, NATIONAL PUBLICITY STUDIOS

72

73

In many New Zealanders' belief, man has never built anything more beautiful than a boat – or more enjoyable. Some of our earliest memories will be of splashing about in the warm shallows, gathering pipi shells along glistening, gently shelving beaches, launching some floating contrivance that was no toy but a dreamboat named for adventure, eating picnic lunch with crusts for the screaming gulls and shivering with delight in surf braved on parental shoulders. The sun and the sand, the sea and its boats are our birthright, for we are a maritime people.

Thousands of us race unsinkable amateur-built seven feet six inch sailboats before we can muster as many years as the boat's length in feet. The Auckland Anniversary Day regatta on January 29th is said to be the largest one day regatta in the world; with over 3,000 pleasure craft from plywood midgets to 60 feet keelers and ocean-going cabin cruisers; topsail and bermuda rig, spinnakers as many-hued as Joseph's coat, ballooning past the flag dressed Naval Base, beating back before sundown, closehauled for the finish, the stowing of gear and the cameraderie of a drop o' the doings.

Boat building was one of the earliest of New Zealand's crafts brought to remarkable finesse in scores of designs. Amateurs build their own craft, often in backyards miles from water: carvel and clinker planked, laminated pressed-wood or fabricated fibreglass; over thirty racing types in our own national designs or built to international standards for world trophy competition. Until recent years all our boats were built of kauri, the unique pine that brought Captain Cook ashore for spars, and which timbered the hundreds of scows and schooners of pioneer days.

Wooden ships and iron men – the saying goes; and New Zealand was developed by them. The kauri stands are now almost all cut out and substitutes must replace it, but for the New Zealander a boat is one of our best excuses for ceasing work for money and working hard for fun.

Tourists bored with the Mediterranean circuit of packed beaches, cafe society and commercial exploitation, have been discovering the solitariness of Turkey's beaches from Antalya to Mersin. New Zealand's long coastline has even more to offer in climate, solitude, variety and accessibility. From sub-tropical Bay of Islands in the north to Hawkes Bay on the East Coast, there is an average of 2,000 hours of sunshine per annum, with sweeping sheltered beaches or ocean rollers for the surf rider. From November to March you can bathe in comfort in the warm Pacific from an unending succession of silver sands, with no dangers from sharks and within easy access of excellent accommodation.

Swimming instruction is part of every school's physical education, and the safe enjoyment of water sports comes early to a people so addicted to messing about in boats.

It is a rarity to find a New Zealander who cannot swim.

82

The Waikato district is one of the richest farming areas in New Zealand. Its grassland management is of the highest standard, its pedigree dairy herds achieve astonishing butterfat output, its Animal Research Station at Ruakura enjoys an international reputation, and the New Zealand Co-operative Dairy Company is the largest organisation of its kind in the world. The progressive outlook of the Waikato Agricultural and Pastoral Association makes its Annual show a major event of the Auckland Province.

The City of Hamilton has an urban population approaching 50,000 and within a forty mile radius of the city live over 180,000 people. The new Municipal Building and Public Library, the recently erected Teachers' Training College and the Waikato Branch of Auckland University reflect the growing stature of the city. With the demise of the old University of New Zealand, and the granting of autonomy to the University of Auckland, early assumption by the Waikato Branch of fuller academic powers and eventual autonomy is the logical outcome of population growth and educational need. Hamilton's fine amenities include a lake for small boat sailing and the reaches of the Waikato River, its fronts tree lined and set out in parks and gardens, an established rowing centre.

This is the sixth city of New Zealand and its largest inland centre, bustling with industrial expansion, State housing developments, excellent shopping facilities and notable schools and colleges. With the nearby charming town of Cambridge it is one of the most attractive centres of the North Island.

Opposite
The Lake, Hamilton.
PHOTOGRAPH, ROBIN SMITH PHOTOGRAPHY

Two views of the Waikato River at Hamilton.

Gisborne was the first landing-place of Captain Cook in 1769 and a monument on the eastern side of the harbour entrance commemorates the occasion. In front of the monument stands a cannon believed to have been jettisoned from Cook's vessel, the "Endeavour", when it went aground on the Great Barrier Reef, off the Queensland coast, in 1770. The cannon was later recovered and forwarded to Gisborne.

Dominating the scene is Kaiti Hill, at the foot of which lies a carved Maori meeting house, Poho-o-rawiri, one of the largest in the country. The Maori people of the East Coast have always had a strong influence upon the course of racial development, often conservatively opposing the official policies of integration with the European community.

The southern extremity of Poverty Bay (inappropriately named by Cook because he was unable to secure food there) is Young Nick's Head after Nicholas Young, the cabin boy on Cook's ship, who first sighted New Zealand. Gisborne itself was named after Sir William Gisborne, Secretary for the Colonies when the township was laid out in 1870.

The prosperity of the district today belies Cook's misnomer: sheep and cattle raising, dairying, fruit growing and vegetable cropping are the chief primary industries, and so fertile are certain coastal areas, and so excellent the climate, that over 60 per cent of New Zealand's maize and sweet corn production comes from the Gisborne district.

The city, with a population of some 25,000, is the principal centre and port, serving also Cook County, an area of nearly 800 square miles, notable for its production of citrus and passion fruit. Known as "The City of Bridges", Gisborne is the largest provincial centre of the east coast of the Auckland Provincial district, a rich pastoral area of more than 3,000 square miles.

Inland lies Lake Waikaremoana, 14 miles long, 21 square miles in area, and with a maximum depth of some 800 feet. It is a mountain retreat of great scenic beauty with a first-class tourist hotel and a major hydro-electric installation. It is reached by road from Rotorua and from Wairoa and lies south of the magnificently rugged Urewera Country.

Opposite
Top. Gisborne from the air.
PHOTOGRAPH, GISBORNE HERALD

Bottom. Lake Waikaremoana.
PHOTOGRAPH, STEELE PHOTOGRAPHY

White Island rises from the depths of the Bay of Plenty, 27 miles off shore; 1,075 feet high, 4 miles in circumference, an active volcanic peak which appears to terminate the thermal belt extending from the heartland of the North Island. From the geysers, boiling streams, steam jets and fumaroles of the Island a giant plume of steam vapour rises at times to 10,000 feet. This is a spectacular activity and is best seen by chartered air flight.

Opposite
White Island.
PHOTOGRAPH, NATIONAL PUBLICITY STUDIOS

The twin cities of Napier and Hastings, both of about 33,000 population, discreetly dispute pre-eminence in the Hawkes Bay district. The pastoral fortunes of this very wealthy farming district rival those of Canterbury. Most of its six million acres are devoted to sheep-raising with upwards of 10,000 acres given over to peach, apple and pear orchards, arable cash cropping and vegetable growing for the district's major canning industry.

Nothing pleases the inhabitants more than to have their province described as "English county" in atmosphere; the area around Hastings does indeed look like an English deer park with its poplar shelter belts, plane tree bordered driveways, oaks, liquid amber and cypress trees, and orchards.

Hastings resembles an English market town with its hundreds of acres of parks and gardens and its two annual rural carnivals – the Blossom Festival and the Highland Games, for Scots are also strong in the district. Cape Kidnappers, the promontory to the south of the curving bay, is a protected gannet colony which should not be missed by the visitor during the nesting season.

Napier is the port and capital city of the province, justified in its claim to be "the Riviera of New Zealand". The Marine Parade is a truly lovely esplanade replete with every holiday amenity, immaculate gardens, floral clock and a simple and dignified War Memorial. Between the two cities, the Game Farm at Greenmeadows is one of the few places where kiwis are raised in captivity. Napier and Hastings have both been virtually rebuilt since the major earthquake of 1931, thus becoming, in many respects, the country's two newest cities.

Opposite
Marine Parade, Napier. ' The Golden Mile ':
finest waterfront amenities in New Zealand.
PHOTOGRAPH, NATIONAL PUBLICITY STUDIOS

93

Above
Characteristic early homestead architecture in Hawkes Bay. Fire has destroyed almost all the notable homes of the district but this remains, near Hastings, as an excellent example of the English country influence so strong in the district's architecture, farming and horticulture.

Opposite
City of Hastings and the Heretaunga Plains looking towards Cape Kidnappers (top left): The most fertile area in New Zealand.

PHOTOGRAPHS by courtesy
J. WATTIE CANNERIES LTD

95

Above
The oldest of the bath houses in Rotorua gardens.
PHOTOGRAPH, ROBIN SMITH PHOTOGRAPHY

Opposite
Boiling mud, Rotorua.

PHOTOGRAPH, ROBIN SMITH PHOTOGRAPHY

Rotorua is a place of geysers, boiling pools and bubbling mud, trout, limpid lakes, steam and Maoris. It is the chief tourist resort of New Zealand's thermal region that stretches in a 20 mile wide belt from the Tongariro National Park to White Island in the Bay of Plenty.

Rotorua township, a well appointed spa with a community devoted to tourist interests, is also the commercial focus of newly developed country and vast exotic forests.

Its many thermal wonders, its beauty, both rugged and tranquil, and its excellent trout fishing make Rotorua one of the most unusual and captivating holiday centres in the country.

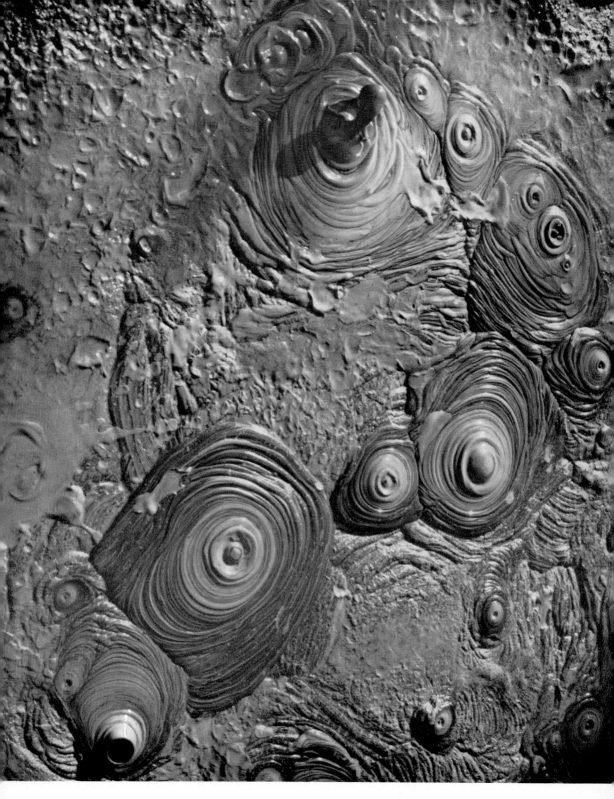

Opposite
Two young Maori girls in native dress stand
before a Rotorua geyser as it blows steam and
boiling water high into the air.
PHOTOGRAPH, STEELE PHOTOGRAPHY

Below
A group of hot mineral pools in their natural
state used for bathing by the Maoris whose
homes on the hill above still retain many
characteristics of their original native dwellings
while taking advantage of more modern
materials.
PHOTOGRAPH, STEELE PHOTOGRAPHY

Mere words can do little justice to New Zealand's cathedral caves. Australia has its Jenolan Caves, vast and magnificent; Kentucky's Mammoth Caves have their Star Chamber, roofed with crystalline formations that glitter in reflected torchlight; the Blue and Green Grottos of Capri are memorable for the pellucid light reflected from the sandy bottom. But there is no similar natural wonder elsewhere to match the ethereal luminescence of Waitomo's Glow-worm grotto, where the stygian darkness is irradiated by myriads of these tiny creatures spangling the arched roof and limestone walls of the great cavern. When they are disturbed by noise, their radiance dims; but to drift silently on the underground river through the Glow-worm Grotto is to have seemingly within reach the Milky Way, an impression sharpened by the absence of sound and the illusion of drifting through space.

To miss this phenomenon while in New Zealand would be like visiting Vatican City and failing to see the Basilica of St Peter illuminated for pontifical vespers.

Opposite
The larva from the egg of the glow-worm fly is between one and two inches long with a segmented transparent body from the tail of which is emitted the greenish blue radiance. The light, which lacks any ultra-violet and almost all heat, is thought to be a by-product of chemical oxidisation. Other creatures have this luminescence, but only in the Waitomo Caves can such a mass display be seen, with each glow-worm in its individual nest using its light to attract for food the tiny midges from the mud of the river below. The absence of wind that would entangle the threads with their glutinous globlets, the freedom from creatures that prey on glow-worms in the open air and the constant temperature and humidity provide ideal breeding conditions for the glow-worms. Despite the appearance of millions, their number in the Grotto is estimated about a hundred thousand. Natural selection keeps the number fairly constant, for both larvae and pupae are eaten by their fellows if they stray from the square-inch of rock surface that is the average area of occupation. The hanging threads seen in the picture are the " fishing lines " hanging from the ceiling which trap the midges attracted by the light of the larvae. The threads themselves are invisible to the insects in the complete darkness of the cave space and are illuminated in the picture by the time exposure necessary to record the scene.

PHOTOGRAPHS, NATIONAL PUBLICITY STUDIOS

The turbulent Aratiatia Rapids lie nine miles north of Taupo on the Waikato, New Zealand's largest river. Four miles south of the Rapids is the Wairakei thermal area with the inferno of the Geyser Valley, and three miles from Taupo the river tumbles over the Huka Falls at the rate of 40,000 gallons per second. Close by is the famed Karapiti Blow Hole, known to the Maoris for at least 600 years.

Although the traveller's urge to reach Taupo is understandable, it would be a pity to miss these striking scenes en route.

Opposite
A stretch of the Aratiatia Rapids looking up-stream towards Lake Taupo.
PHOTOGRAPH, MARILYN McKENZIE

Fishermen's tales in New Zealand are of "Leviathan drawn out with a hook". From the most famous fishing centre, Lake Taupo, anglers take some *500 tons* of trout each year; yet Taupo is only one of literally hundreds of waters from which probably more trout between five and ten pounds have been taken than all the rest of the world put together. The regulations require that anything under 14 inches be thrown back, and rainbow trout have been caught weighing 25 pounds and brown trout up to 30 pounds.

Anglers from the world's famed countries have confirmed that New Zealand's Atlantic and quinnat salmon similarly attain size and fighting qualities greater than in their native habitat. Forty pounders are far too common to trouble a taxidermist's art. The fresh water angler may for a nominal licence fee fish anywhere in New Zealand's secluded streams and tumbling river reaches for a full season. In certain lakes, all year angling is permitted: Lake Tutira in Hawkes Bay, for example.

Opposite,

PHOTOGRAPH, STEELE PHOTOGRAPHY

Overleaf
Two trout fishing scenes.
PHOTOGRAPHS. NATIONAL PUBLICITY STUDIOS

In big-game fishing, our American friends concede us the finest sport they know, coming year after year to the fishing grounds that stretch from North Cape to the Bay of Plenty: 300 miles of coastal waters dedicated to the ritual of bringing man and marlin together in fighting mood.

In 1959 it was a New Zealander who caught the world record blue marlin at the Hawaiian International Fishing Contest, using a 24 thread line with a breaking strain of 80 pounds. His fish weighed 444 pounds. In 1960 an American sportsman repaid the compliment by coming to New Zealand's Otehei Bay, where with the same type tackle he took a new world's record blue marlin weighing 462 pounds. Year by year the records tumble, for our broadbill, black and striped marlin, mako, thresher and hammer-head sharks are all tremendous fighters.

Below
The beginning of a battle . . .

Opposite
 . . . and the end.
PHOTOGRAPHS, NATIONAL PUBLICITY STUDIOS

Palmerston North, a city of about 44,000 people, and the commercial centre for the Manawatu district, is fortunate in its many public parks and gardens. The largest is the Botanical Gardens of 361 acres, with the Begonia house, Aviary, children's playing area and the famed Cherry Blossom Drive. The central feature of the city, the Square, has its 17 acres laid out in trees, shrubs, fountains and ponds. Ablaze with seasonal flowers Palmerston North is a memorable sight.

Massey Agricultural College, a world-famed research centre, was the logical choice for the site of New Zealand's new Veterinary School. Within $2\frac{1}{2}$ miles of the Square, its beautiful grounds cover 50 acres; the farms comprise 1,250 acres at the College and two additional properties, one 8 miles distant, the other in Southern Hawkes Bay. Degree courses are given in Agriculture, Horticulture and Dairy Technology, and diploma courses in Dairy Farming Sheep Farming, Dairy Manufactures, Horticulture, Wool, and Wool Classing.

The Dairy Research Institute, situated at Massey College, is the national dairy research organisation, specialising in the problems of milk production, the manufacture of dairy produce, and the design of farm machinery.

Also associated with Massey College is the Grasslands Division of the Department of Scientific and Industrial Research, concerned with the improvement of the pasture grasses and clovers which are the green gold of New Zealand. These are the basic researches upon which the entire national economy relies for the development of more intensive farming, improved bloodstock and pasture management.

Palmerston North University College has already widened its organisation since its foundation in 1960 as a constituent College of the Victoria University of Wellington with only the Departments of Education, English, History, Mathematics and Modern Languages, mainly for extra-mural studies. Its growth as a centre of higher education in this prosperous district must lead naturally to autonomy.

Opposite
Looking across the town square and gardens, Palmerston North: the peace memorial in the foreground.
PHOTOGRAPH, ROBIN SMITH PHOTOGRAPHY

Wanganui is one of the ancient areas of Maori settlement, and an early source of food supplies to the colonists at Wellington. Wanganui was established in 1840 on land grants haphazardly negotiated by Edward Jerningham Wakefield which were soon vigorously repudiated by the Maoris. The early years were therefore marked by strife, and finally warfare, and at one time Governor Fitzroy urged the pioneers to abandon the township. Determined to remain, they were reinforced by troops and for a quarter century stockades dominated the scene at the mouth of this beautiful Wanganui River. The troubled times passed, the legacy of loyalty from the Maoris at Putiki enriched the expansion which followed; good relations between the two races have been a strong factor in the subsequent development of the district. Today, Wanganui, with its urban population of upwards of 36,000 is one of the truly characteristic cities of New Zealand. Its Observatory contains the largest telescope in the Dominion.

Opposite
Jerusalem, an early Maori mission station on the Wanganui River.
PHOTOGRAPH, MANNERING & DONALDSON LTD.

Whatever Aucklanders may say, Wellington is the capital city of New Zealand and not to be evaluated in mere terms of its population of 145,000 (to which should be added the 100,000 of the Hutt Valley). Here too is a magnificent harbour, fine commercial buildings, head offices of most major enterprises, the newest and busiest airport, the seat of Government, and the only cable-cars in New Zealand.

Not even Manhattan Island was purchased cheaper than Wellington the site of which changed hands in return for beads, jew's harps, clothing, muskets, tomahawks and other trivia; not even Kowloon across the harbour of Hong Kong looks more magical at night than this City of the Hills bespangled by its myriad lights; not even San Francisco has a finer marine drive than Wellington's 28 miles around the foreshore. Wellington's peal of 49 bells is the only carillon in New Zealand.

Here is the country's only floating dock; the largest railway station whose five storeys have a floor area of 51 acres, the first municipality in the world to undertake complete milk treatment and distribution services, one of the largest wooden buildings in the world, the first New Zealand city to install electricity, and a satellite industrial city which courteously confines itself ten miles away.

The National Thoroughbred Sales, held at Trentham every January, show where the centre of gravity really lies – for Australia no less than New Zealand. The Alexander Turnbull Library has a world-wide reputation for its collections of books, maps and manuscripts of the Pacific area, and its resources in English literature are unrivalled in the Southern Hemisphere. The National Art Gallery and the Dominion Museum house excellent collections of European art and Polynesian culture. The General Assembly Library is the largest in the country.

The Hutt Valley, at first given over to agricultural and pastoral farming serving the needs of the city, has increasingly become a major industrial centre. Lower Hutt, merely a village at the turn of the century with about 2,000 population, has now a heavy concentration of commercial and industrial life and a population of about 55,000. The municipalities of Petone, Lower Hutt and Upper Hutt are outside the administration of Wellington City, but with it form one urban community. Petone is the site of the original settlement of 1840; Lower Hutt possesses the most impressive civic centre of any New Zealand city, and northwards to Upper Hutt lie the greatest concentration of State houses and municipal amenities in the country; motor-car assembly works, the railway workshops, bulk oil installations, engineering foundries, paint, biscuits, footwear, radio and electrical factories have changed what was once the dormitory suburb of the capital into the fifth city of New Zealand.

114

Below
Beautiful Wellington harbour and the city seen
from the Tinakori Hills.
PHOTOGRAPH, NATIONAL PUBLICITY STUDIOS

Above
Castlepoint, on the east coast of the Wairarapa
district, Wellington Province.
PHOTOGRAPH, D. S. McLACHLAN

Opposite
Top. Parliament Buildings, Wellington.
PHOTOGRAPH, NATIONAL PUBLICITY STUDIOS

Bottom. Lower Hutt Town Hall seen from
across Riddiford Park.
PHOTOGRAPH by courtesy of
LOWER HUTT BOROUGH COUNCIL

Rugby football began on that historic occasion when a player at Rugby School, in England, breached the rules by picking up the ball and running with it, instead of playing it only with the foot. In the subsequent evolution of the game, New Zealand has for half a century been periodically supreme among the rugby playing nations. This sport is the first choice of every boy sufficiently robust or fleet of foot; the winter season of play is organised in grade competitions from primary schools through universities, and in the adult community through club, provincial and national Test teams. Known in international Tests as the "All Blacks" from the colour of their jerseys, shorts and socks, New Zealand Rugby representatives usually include members of the Maori race, which has produced some superb players.

The New Zealand character and temperament declare themselves on the football field where almost every boy in every generation runs the gauntlet of rugby. Those who believe that New Zealanders are becoming soft in their welfare society might reflect that the nearest approach to hero worship is accorded the Rugby international player.

In these two scenes are recorded the climactic moments of the game, the scoring of a try and the kick at goal.

Opposite
The famed Don Clarke, who is the highest scoring goal-kicker in rugby history, demonstrates his prodigious boot at a schoolboy practice.
PHOTOGRAPH, THE AUCKLAND STAR

Overleaf
The scoring of a try in an international match.
PHOTOGRAPH, THE AUCKLAND STAR

118

119

Three hundred and twenty years ago the Dutch navigator Abel Tasman dropped anchor in Golden Bay, Nelson, and named the new country Staten Land, thinking it was part of the legendary southern continent which the Dutch East India Company had sent him to discover.

Here, Tasman had four of his ship's company killed by the Maoris, so that he named it Murderers' Bay — an injustice to so beautiful a place later corrected by the more appropriate title of Golden Bay.

By 1850, Nelson was the second most important town in New Zealand, according to the records of the N.Z. Company, which gave the following population figures for that year:

Wellington 5,479 : Nelson 4,047 : New Plymouth 1,412 : Otago 1,482 : Canterbury 301. Auckland is not mentioned at all!

In 1958, Nelson achieved the status of a city; today with a population of 26,000 it is notable as a holiday centre for its abundant sunshine, its mountain, river and lake scenery, and its quietude.

Nelson has New Zealand's only commercial tobacco growing industry; over 3 thousand acres are planted and a yearly crop of 5,000,000 pounds weight of leaf is harvested. Nelson is also the largest apple and pear growing area in the country; 3,000 acres of apple orchards, and 3,500 acres of pip fruits. All the hops used in New Zealand brewing come from the district; and in a country of heavy afforestation, Nelson has the largest area of close on 3,000,000 acres of timber trees. The scenic routes from Nelson to Westport and Greymouth are magnificent, both the coastal route through the Buller Gorge, and the inland route through rugged mountain country.

Opposite
Top. The road through the Weka Pass, North Canterbury.
PHOTOGRAPH, ROBIN SMITH PHOTOGRAPHY

Bottom. Apple orchards, Redwood Valley, Nelson.
PHOTOGRAPH, NATIONAL PUBLICITY STUDIOS

The City of Christchurch and indeed the whole province of Canterbury reflect the fact that this was the last and most successful colonising project inspired by Edward Gibbon Wakefield and his New Zealand Company. The Canterbury Association, founded in 1848, was an attempt to found a model Church of England settlement, by selecting immigrants from all classes to represent an exclusively English section of society transplanted to New Zealand.

Within six months after the 'first four ships' arrived at Lyttelton in December 1850, a small township had sprung up on the plains; this was named Christchurch after the Oxford College of John Robert Godley, leader of the Association. The original plan of small cropping the plains was abandoned as Canterbury began to find its wealth in sheep raising on the most extensive natural grassland in New Zealand.

The influence of these 'Canterbury Pilgrims' is evident today in the huge Hagley Park – the green heart of the city; in the winding River Avon, its banks laid out in lawns carpeted with spring flowers and its shallow waters crossed by many bridges; in the ecclesiastical Gothic-Revival architecture of so many public buildings, and the Cathedral Square at the heart of it all.

In a century Christchurch's population has grown from 3,000 to almost 220,000. Some four million carcasses of prime Canterbury lamb and mutton go annually to the United Kingdom; high grade wool, wheat, barley, pasture seed and green crops show the fertility of the plains. Industry is also strong in Christchurch, which has its woollen mills, freezing works, meat processing plants, chemical and fertiliser works, felt and textile works and engineering workshops.

Opposite
Hagley Park, Christchurch with the River Avon seen from Armagh Street Bridge. In the background are buildings of Christ's College (secondary school).
PHOTOGRAPH, NATIONAL PUBLICITY STUDIOS

Laid out in rectangular pattern, the city streets bear the names of English bishoprics; the Cathedral (designed by Sir Gilbert Scott) is claimed to be the finest Gothic style church in the Dominion, its peal of ten bells being a duplicate of the upper ten in St Paul's Cathedral, London. The river is not named after England's Avon; two Scots were there before the Canterbury Pilgrims arrived, and the Deans brothers named it for a small stream near their family home in Lanarkshire. It is popularly held that the willows that fringe the Avon were propagated from cuttings taken from the grave of Napoleon on St Helena. From these was grown the first willow at the French settlement of Akaroa, and this tree, it is said, supplied the cuttings planted along the river banks in Christchurch.

Until 1876, Canterbury was administered by its own Provincial Government; the Gothic character of the fine Provincial Chamber reflects again ecclesiastical influence adapted to secular purposes; and the building remains as a striking example of architectural dignity, despite the seeming incongruities of much of the ornamentation. Canterbury University numbers amongst its distinguished alumni Lord Rutherford of Nelson, pioneer of atomic research. Christchurch airport, close to the city centre, shows, in its international appointments and spacious planning, the strong corporate spirit of the province.

Lincoln Agricultural College, centre of the Wool Research Centre of New Zealand, and situated 14 miles from Christchurch, is noted for its fine flocks of stud sheep and its pedigree herds of Aberdeen Angus cattle. It supervises the management of some 50 farms in Canterbury in addition to its own 1,264 acres of farmlands.

127

Above
The terminal building at Christchurch's new
international airport.
PHOTOGRAPH, MANNERING &
                    DONALDSON LTD.

Opposite
Interior of the old Provincial Parliamentary
Chambers in Christchurch.
PHOTOGRAPH, NATIONAL PUBLICITY STUDIOS

Two characteristically English scenes from Canterbury.

Left. Winter in the Mt Cook area.
PHOTOGRAPH, ROBIN SMITH PHOTOGRAPHY

Right. Spring on the River Avon, Christchurch.
PHOTOGRAPH, NATIONAL PUBLICITY STUDIOS

Is there any other country where introduced deer are now so numerous and their foraging so damaging to sapling growth that they are classified as noxious animals and professional cullers are paid a high bounty? In New Zealand, hunting is unrestricted, some 100,000 deer being shot each year, about half of them by amateur sportsmen. The hunter pays no fees, needs no licence, and is involved in no costly safari. New Zealand Deerstalkers' Association supplies the visitor with rifles, ammunition and a guide – all for a modest fee. In this country one may hunt wapiti, moose, Asian thar, chamois, Scottish red deer, elk and spotted deer, Javan rusa, samba stags of up to 700 pounds, Manchurian sika and the New Zealand wild pig.

The principal game birds available in season include duck, pheasant, geese and Californian quail, though to the New Zealander the last would hardly seem fair game. With no snakes or carnivorous animals this country is a happy hunting ground indeed.

The views overleaf are of shooters and pack horses in the Arawhata Valley, South Westland. There are goats and pigs in this area but deer infest the towering back country, as may be seen from the accompanying picture of a magnificent 18 pointer red deer head and skin. Three days' shooting in this valley have loaded the pack horses with skins to the value of £150.

Opposite
Bringing home the whole trophy in the gorge of the Waimakiriri River, Canterbury.

PHOTOGRAPH, MANNERING & DONALDSON LTD.

Overleaf
The more traditional methods.

PHOTOGRAPHS, NATIONAL PUBLICITY STUDIOS

133

135

A New Zealand invention now widely produced in the United States, the Hamilton Turbocraft has the enormous advantage of operating without a propeller. Its motive power comes from the expulsion of a jet of water, enabling the shallow draft craft to operate in the shallowest of rapids and with astonishing power. Not without justification, the Turbocraft has been called the 'almost-no-water boat'.

Here a New Zealand built craft skims across the shallow shingle beds of the Waimakiriri River.

PHOTOGRAPH, MANNERING &
DONALDSON LTD.

With a population of some 27,000 Timaru is the second city of Canterbury, halfway between Christchurch and Dunedin, and the gateway to the high country of South Canterbury and the Southern Alps. Timaru was the first town in New Zealand to institute a town-planning scheme. The artificial harbour with a breakwater 3,000 feet long is one of the best secondary harbours in the Dominion, with the incidental gain of lovely Caroline Bay with its gently shelving sweep of beach, backed by lawns and gardens. This port, commercial centre and holiday city serves a tract of rich hinterland noted for its production of wool, wheat, barley and small seed. Flour, woollen and knitwear mills; footwear, biscuit and macaroni factories; freezing works, breweries and linen flax production constitute the principal industries of South Canterbury. Timaru's museum is a treasure-house of early colonial history.

It is estimated that the rivers and lakes of the district afford some 500 miles of fishing waters, Lake Alexandrina being noted for its brown and rainbow trout (brown trout up to 17 lb. are caught on the fly) and Lake MacGregor also offers excellent sport with artificial bait or lure. Quinnat salmon run in the Opihi river and every season between January and April hundreds of fine fish are landed – often up to 20 and 30 lbs.

Fortyeight miles from Geraldine, in Ashburton County, lies the famous Mesopotamia Station, first owned by Samuel Butler, the 19th century author of 'The Way of All Flesh' and the satirical novel 'Erewhon'. Butler, who arrived in Canterbury in 1860, built his hut near Forest Creek, and later a sod cottage near the present homestead. It was an incongruous affair, with a grand piano hauled in by bullock dray for the consolation of a cultivated man who, with no knowledge of farming when he arrived, nevertheless managed to double his capital in a few years before returning to England. This is historic country, indeed.

Opposite
Caroline Bay, Timaru, with the harbour in the background.
PHOTOGRAPH, NATIONAL PUBLICITY STUDIOS

139

Though it was originally to have been named New Edinburgh, the Scots settlers called it Dunedin, the old Celtic name for Scotland's capital city. On the nearby peninsula was the Maori village of Otakou, corrupted by the early whalers to "Otago" – now the name of the whole province of 8 million acres of farmland, lake and mountain scenery.

Dunedin, with a population approaching 105,000 is a leading academic centre, with its National Schools of Medicine, Dentistry, Technology, Home Science, Physiotherapy, Physical Education, its Hocken Library and its Museum. The Scottish tradition is strong almost a century after it was constituted a City in 1865 and the burr persists in third generation descendants of the Scottish Freechurchmen founders.

Otago and Southland between them have more than 11 million sheep, almost a quarter of the country's total number; the woollen mills in Dunedin, Mosgiel, Oamaru and Milton provide a large proportion of the country's clothing needs; the New Zealand Wool Industries Research Institute has its headquarters in Dunedin, and Otago's wool clip has increased 41 per cent in the last seven years as a result of its researches.

The discovery of gold in Central Otago in 1861 by Gabriel Read made Dunedin the first financial centre of the young country. In the first four years of the "strike", gold to the value of £7,000,000 was exported. Commerce and industry flourished. The city soon became the leader in civic development; gas lighting was introduced in 1863; water was laid on in 1867, and by 1879, the country's first tramcars, both horse-drawn and steam, were running, and it was in Dunedin that the first electric trams were introduced in 1900. Within three years the general change over to electricity had been made; it was Dunedin's successful operation of the hydro-electric station at Waipori in 1907 that prompted the Government to undertake the generation of hydro-electric supply on a national basis.

In education, the Scots also gave New Zealand a lead; in 1869 the Otago Provincial Council passed an ordinance founding a University of Otago; other centres later established University Colleges, but not until 1957 were they entitled Universities. In 1907, the New Zealand Society for the Health of Women and Children (the Plunket Society) was founded in Dunedin and has influenced child care programmes in many parts of the world.

141

New Zealand's first consignment of frozen mutton was shipped to London from Port Chalmers in the sailing ship "Dunedin" in 1882. From that beginning, refrigerated exports have determined the wealth and prosperity of New Zealand; today Otago kills some three million sheep each year for the markets of the world.

Three quarters of New Zealand's apricot trees are in Otago, and produce 200,000 bushels a year, more than a third of this output is processed in Otago canneries. About half the country's nectarine orchards, a third of its plum and a quarter of the peach orchards are located in Otago, providing an annual crop of about 200,000 bushels.

Culturally, Dunedin has a special character; the Art Gallery possesses a notable collection of oils and a fine selection of English water colours; the Museum is specially strong in its Polynesian and Egyptian sections; and the dignified Gothic of its architecture is a delight. Mellowed age is Dunedin's characteristic.

Above
Queenstown, Lake Wakatipu. View from Ben Lomond, the Lombardy poplars turning to gold, the first snows of autumn mantling the Remarkables: an incomparable panorama of lake, forest and mountain scenery.
PHOTOGRAPH, NATIONAL PUBLICITY STUDIOS

Opposite
The Dunedin Railway Station, a fine example of early architecture.
PHOTOGRAPH, EVENING STAR NEWSPAPER

143

Invercargill, southernmost city in the British Commonwealth, is the chief city of Southland province, with a population nearing 42,000. Its wide streets, named after Scottish rivers; its attractive gardens; its airport, close to the city and terminal of the main trunk air services; and its proximity to the deep water port of Bluff make Invercargill one of the fastest developing centres of New Zealand. Southland province has some of the richest farming land in the South Island, and the traveller cannot fail to note the air of good thrift in the homesteads.

The province has a thousand miles of trout fishing waters, many magnificent lakes and all the fiords, northernmost of which is Milford Sound. The walking track from Lake Te Anau – a 3 day hike of 33 miles – is renowned as "the finest walk in the world"; but Milford Track is but one of the many ways of seeing the beauty of the fiords which lace the western coast of Southland for 120 miles.

Below
Deep water port of Bluff. Under a £5,000,000 development scheme a new harbour, shown here under construction, has been built to accommodate the largest overseas vessels.
PHOTOGRAPH, HAZELDINE'S STUDIOS LTD

Opposite
Mount Cook, Southern Alps.
PHOTOGRAPH, STEELE PHOTOGRAPHY

What is in other countries the rich man's pastime, is in New Zealand cheaply available for all. Snow sports are pursued in both Islands, some ski grounds affording unobstructed runs of 3,500 vertical feet. Ski-tows have been established and chair-lifts operate at Chateau Tongariro, where luxury accommodation is an alternative to the simplicity of alpine huts higher up the mountain slope.

The exploits of our international climbing teams are well enough known but nothing can really prepare the visitor for the splendour of New Zealand's alpine regions. This country owes its tourist attractions not to man but to nature; one is never far from the hills and mountains towering above the plains, and the flight from Wellington to Christchurch down the east coast of the South Island must be said to parallel anywhere in the world. The coastal plain is chequered in the same pattern as that of the English farm land and to the west the dazzling snow-clad splendour of the central alps stands sentinel in sharpest contrast. Excellent motoring roads connect all the mountain resorts to the cities and airports, so that within hours the visitor may be ski-ing, climbing or warmly ensconced in a hotel lounge overlooking it all.

Opposite
Mitre Peak (5,560 ft.) Milford Sound.
PHOTOGRAPH, MARILYN McKENZIE

Below
Tutoko Peak (9,042 ft.) near Milford Sound.
PHOTOGRAPH, STEELE PHOTOGRAPHY

150

Opposite
Mount Cook (12,349 ft.) as seen from halfway
up the Ball Pass ski run.
PHOTOGRAPH, NATIONAL PUBLICITY STUDIOS

Below
Fox Glacier, Westland. The main ice fall of
the Fox from Chancellor Ridge (top left corner)
a low peak of Haast.
PHOTOGRAPH, NATIONAL PUBLICITY STUDIOS

Above

The " T " bar tow on Staircase slope, Mount Ruapehu with the Staircase Shop (centre) and Ruapehu Ski Club's Lodge (background).

PHOTOGRAPH, NATIONAL PUBLICITY STUDIOS

Opposite

The knife edge of Mount Sefton (10,359 ft.) as seen by a skier on the Ball Pass. One of the most famous down hill championship racing courses starts near this point and descends thousands of feet to near the junction of the Ball and Tasman Glaciers. Mount Cook area, Southern Alps.

PHOTOGRAPH, NATIONAL PUBLICITY STUDIOS

Overleaf

Ski-ing, Tongariro National Park. This jump, taken in the middle of a downhill run on the slopes of Mount Ruapehu (9,175 ft.) is photographed against the background of Mount Ngauruhoe (7,515 ft.) one of New Zealand's active volcanoes. The Chateau, most noted mountain hotel in the North Island, lies on the lower slopes of Mount Ruapehu.

PHOTOGRAPH, NATIONAL PUBLICITY STUDIOS

156

157

159

At the turn of the century there were in New Zealand 372 thousand dairy cows: today there are over 2 million; a direct result of top-dressing (the spreading of fertiliser on existing pasture swards) much of which is now done by aircraft, renewal by fresh sowing, better quality grasses, the provision of electricity and labour-saving machines support prices and farm diversification.

The total cattle population is round about 6 million of which over 5 million are in the North Island. Dairy cows are predominantly the Jersey breed. These amount to about 85% of the total.

The total number of pigs would be something less than three quarters of a million.

Above
A view of typical rolling Taranaki grasslands overlcoked by Mount Egmont.
PHOTOGRAPH. STEELE PHOTOGRAPHY

Opposite
Harvesting pedigree perennial rye grass and white clover: threshing the ripened swath in gently rolling country around Hazelburn, South Canterbury.
PHOTOGRAPH, NATIONAL PUBLICITY STUDIOS

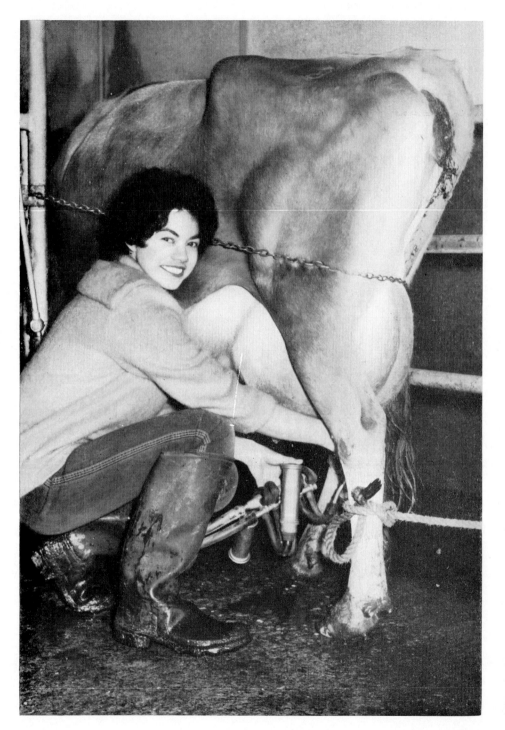

162

Opposite
PHOTOGRAPH, DONALD POYNTON

Below
PHOTOGRAPH, STEELE PHOTOGRAPHY

166

Sheep are raised from one end of New Zealand to the other with more than 30 million breeding ewes in a total sheep population of over 47 million, representing a wide range of breeds and crosses.

With so much of the national economy dependent upon sheep it is not surprising that the world champion shearer should be a New Zealander. In 1960 Mr Godfrey Bowen, as an officer of the New Zealand Wool Board demonstrating his technique of machine shearing in the United Kingdom, established a new world record by catching and shearing 559 sheep in 9 hours. They were Welsh mountain animals, small and bare in the points, in a country where shepherds cherish every animal and where no blood must be drawn if one wishes to leave town safely. Under unbelieving eyes, with a 5 minute break every hour for an official count, the New Zealander – and his 559 sheep – emerged unscathed from a trial by ordeal that is not likely to be bettered save by the Bowen method. When it was over the locals admitted grudgingly that any man who could handle that number of wild Welsh breeds without getting his head kicked off could doubtless shear a rhinoceros – if it grew wool.

The visitor to New Zealand can see any number of operators using the same machines and the Bowen methods, working as he does blindfolded if necessary. For long enough, the world record has alternated between the Bowen Brothers, though Godfrey has now stated that he has bowed out from the record scene. Sheep men the world over refuse to believe that such figures can be handled, and the burly Bowen has been manoevred into demonstrations with animals which he says "are almost as big as Shetland ponies".

Opposite
Yarded merino hoggets at Glentanner Station. This station is at the head of Lake Pukaki and the stock are grazed in the high country of the Ben Ohau and Sealy Ranges including the lower slopes of Mount Cook.
PHOTOGRAPH, NATIONAL PUBLICITY STUDIOS

Below. Virgin forest land; in the background Mount Tasman, Mount Cook and the Franz Josef Glacier (centre).

Opposite. Giant Totara trees in the native forests west of Lake Taupo.

N.Z. FOREST SERVICE PHOTOGRAPHS by J. H. Johns, A.R.P.S.

Whereas the noble kauri is confined chiefly to the north of New Zealand, the totara is more widespread and attains almost the same lofty height. These are the two kings of our forests. The kauri grows often a 60 foot bole without a lateral branch, straight grained, supple and durable. A thousand years it takes to mature, and the visitor may see two magnificent stands, the best at Waipoua State Forest Reserve, its noblest specimens but saplings when William the Conqueror built his wooden castle at Windsor. Kauri gum, its hard, amber like resinous sap, was once sought by the varnishmaker and is now a collector's curiosity.

The angular and untidy head of the totara, rears from a massive trunk which provided the primitive Maori with his great canoes up to 70 feet in length. Its oily timber was ideal too for the intricate carving on the tekoteko that surmounted his rooftree, and for the symbolic lintels of his doorway, carved with stone-age tools in grotesque figures and spiral motifs. A fine totara tree was therefore a tribal heirloom, passed from chieftain to son, and finally felled with religous ceremony from the tohunga, the medicine man of the tribe. The Maori was an animist, peopling every great tree with a spirit, benign or mischievous so that interference with a forest god was not to be undertaken lightly or inadvertently.

Opposite
Pine forests showing the Waikato River and hydro station at Atiamuri. These trees are part of what are said to be the largest man-made forests in the world.
PHOTOGRAPH, NATIONAL PUBLICITY STUDIOS

The rimu or red pine is still the general utility timber in this land of wooden homes. Anyone who can recognise these three characteristic members of our forest family – kauri, totara and rimu – will have the key to much of New Zealand's history, industry, domestic building and timber resources. Two other trees are an essential part of our life: the pohutukawa of the coastline, whose blood-red blossom heralds the Christmas season and whose tough timber is keenly sought for knees in small boat construction; and the kowhai – scarlet or yellow – whose blossoming was the ancient Maori's almanac by which he planted the kumara, the sweet potato of Polynesia.

Among the exotics we have borrowed, the Australian wattle transforms many a New Zealand driveway into a golden road to Samarkand; the hawthorn hedges of the quiet countryside are redolent of England; the rhododendrons that flourish in our soil and climate are nostalgic for the South African, and the oleanders that grow to twenty feet in diameter remind us how Mediterranean are our out-door conditions.

It was once said that England is an island largely composed of coal deposits and surrounded by fish, yet government had managed to make both coal and fish scarce and costly. Somewhat more fairly it can be said of New Zealand that the price of fish reflects the occupational hazards of this industry, since nothing can reduce the discomforts and potential dangers of operating up to 400 miles from base in motor vessels of between 40 and 60 feet. Commercial fishing is a small industry.

Recently, however, the penetration of Japanese fishing vessels into the coastal waters of New Zealand shows that if we will not capitalise these resources, others will.

New Zealand was opened by the whalers of the late 18th and early 19th centuries. As early as 1792 a Sydney vessel left a gang of sealers at Dusky Sound, and the first whaling ships hunted the sperm whale in New Zealand waters under American and French as well as British captains. The whaling industry had by 1830 set up twenty shore establishments, mostly in the South Island, served by vessels under New Englanders from Salem and Nantucket, polyglot crews from Port Jackson, Australia, and Frenchmen from Tahiti.

In recent years an indigenous whaling industry has been operating successfully, for the modern world still has uses for whale oil. The whaling station operates in the Marlborough Sound, but is only of minor importance with catches of less than 200 humpbacks in an average season.

The search for shark oil has the side advantage of reducing these enemies of the commercial catch whilst providing liver oil for the pharmaceutical industry.

Opposite
A vessel of the crayfishing fleet operating in West Coast waters, the *Dolphin*, from Greymouth, is seen here steaming up to the head of Milford Sound to shelter from bad weather in
PHOTOGRAPH, NATIONAL PUBLICITY STUDIOS

Harrison's Cove. This is easier than the long run back to their home port and beneath the fiord's towering heights vessels may ride out any storm in safety.

Above
Fisherman enjoy a well-earned break aboard a shark fishing boat on the Kaipara Harbour, Northland.
PHOTOGRAPH, THE AUCKLAND STAR

Opposite
A whale chaser operating in Cook Strait out from the Marlborough Sounds.
PHOTOGRAPH, THE AUCKLAND STAR

The thermal area, extending from Rotorua through Wairakei and Taupo to the active volcano of Ngauruhoe, has its special fascination. This is the heartland of the North Island; pumice country, planted forests, rivers, lakes and waterfalls; eerie with its plumes of emitted steam, boiling mud, hot pools; ancient home of famous warrior tribes.

The thermal waters, chiefly of Rotorua and Te Aroha, have their therapeutic triumphs. The modern medical unit for rheumatic disorders at Queen Elizabeth Hospital, Rotorua, administers the full spa treatment. Rotorua may not be as extensively thermal as Yellowstone National Park, but it concentrates every conceivable phenomenon within its sulphurous scope. It abounds in hot springs for bathing, of both acid and alkali type; carbonated thermal waters; mud of fascinating texture for beauty treatment; pyretic or vapour baths for hydrotherapy. The arthritic are tenderly handled by specialists, whose relief of pain and stiffness is a source of wonder to those who have never felt a twinge. Athletes, sportsmen and tired farmers alike vouch for their efficacy.

New Zealanders do not "drink the waters" as do visitors to the European spas – perhaps because we are not yet a liverish nation; yet devotees declare that our New Zealand mineral waters do have unusual content; iodine springs at Morere, mercurial springs at Ngawha, mercurial mud at Ohaeawai. Mercury, sulphur and iodine have been much used the world over in the treatment of certain skin disorders and chronic inflammation. Though there is no cult of thermalism in this country, we are as well equipped as anywhere in the world to cater for these needs. Every visitor should at least discover the bathing pools of Rotorua, balm to the skin of the fair sex and sedative to the tired business man.

There is no sleep like that which follows the deep therapy of Rotorua's Ward Baths – something that can be put to the test for a shilling or two.

Opposite
Top. A general view of the geothermal valley at Wairakei. The tourist hotel can be seen in the foreground.

Bottom left. A steep ascent in the 20-inch steam mains piping the thermal steam to the generators.

Bottom right. The unusual warning sign on the main highway at Wairakei.

PHOTOGRAPHS, NATIONAL PUBLICITY STUDIOS

184

185

At the laying of the foundation stone of the new Napier Cathedral – replacing that which was destroyed in the severe earthquake of 1931 – a Maori lay preacher from Whangara is about to present an elaborately carved whaka-huia containing a thousand pounds, the donations from Maori pastorates. The dignity and reverential humility of the Christian Maori, caught so naturally in this picture are representative of the true spirit of the native race which produces many bishops and clergy of eminence. The Maori is by tradition a mystic, with spiritual perceptions of great enrichment to the ideals of New Zealand life and thought. Whether his ancient polytheism has been adapted to Christian theology, or continues to follow the distinctive forms of Maori religion, it is a deep stream in the personal and community life of the Maori people. Such politico-religious faiths as Ratanism and the Ringatu faith continue side by side with Mormon groups and orthodox forms of Christianity. This sectarianism is no less a source of weakness in the Maori witness than it is in the European society. What is generally overlooked is the fact that the Maori people have made such profound adjustments to European life and thought to the advantage of both races. Nowhere is the respect due to these achievements more evident than in the place accorded Maori religious leaders.

The art of carving dominated the cultural life of the ancient Maori: thus he adorned the prow, hull and tailpiece of his canoe, his steering oar and water balers; he carved the entrances to his palisaded villages, his important meeting houses, food stores, treasure chests, and burial places; he carved the gourd from which he drank, the vessels that held his food, his tools and his musical instruments; he even carved h'mself – his face, waist and legs – by tattooing. Never entirely lost, the skill of the Maori is today taking new forms of expression, of which this recent piece of sculpture in native white pine is an illuminating example. The work of a Maori headmaster of a Hawkes Bay primary school, it is entitled "An English Gentleman". It reveals the droll humour no less than the new sophistication of the Maori mind in its satirical treatment of the English overlord of the last century, at whom Maori culture has lived to laugh and sees now in perspective.

PHOTOGRAPHS, RUSSELL ORR LTD

The Report of the Parry Committee on New Zealand universities (December 1959) sought to analyse the relationship between the university's role and the community's aspiration, and stated:

"At the moment New Zealand's attitude towards its universities and colleges is similar to that of most other young and developing countries, not far removed from a pioneer tradition which is prepared to cater for the needs of today and tomorrow but doubts the value of planning too far ahead, and which tends to prefer practice without theory. To say this is not to be critical of the pioneer tradition in its time and place, but to doubt whether the continuance of that tradition will longer serve New Zealand's needs in a world where scientific, social and technological changes have become the norm, and where planning ahead is as accepted a part of public policy as it is personal policy".

Itemising the five urgent problems requiring solution in university expansion in this country – staffing, buildings, conditions of study, university government, and finance – the Report made recommendations under all five heads, some of which are already being implemented and all of which remain as the challenge to New Zealand higher education.

These pictures show the evolution of university architecture, from left to right, Otago (the oldest,) Canterbury, Victoria and Auckland (the newest) with each of the four centres now re-building its university, the outward face no less than the inner spirit is 'set for change"

PHOTOGRAPHS, NATIONAL PUBLICITY STUDIOS

About 17 miles south of Westport, the commercial centre of Buller County, lies Charleston, probably the most interesting of the gold-rush settlements which have since almost disappeared. This was no mere 'canvas town' that flourished for a few hectic years, but a busy metropolis with library, newspaper, hospital, 3 banks, 80 licensed hotels, theatres, and a direct shipping service with Australia. Gold was discovered nearby in August 1866 and 1,200 diggers arrived by the end of the year: within 3 years there were 12,000. For 7 years Charleston maintained its reputation as one of the richest fields on the Coast, but as the gold was worked out the population slowly dwindled. By the turn of the century the last of the 80 large crushing and sluicing claims had closed and the demolition gangs were at work. Visitors today can form little idea of the magnitude of the early diggings. Square miles of country were worked over to a depth of from 6 to 20 feet. The old European Hotel, opened in 1876 by Charles Weitzel, has been a solitary landmark for many years, and with its false front it is reminiscent of the saloons of America's cow towns – and of the movie sets which seek to re-create them. It is the last of the famed 80 hotels, still standing amidst the newer, more decorous community that nowadays works the coal deposits by open-cast methods.

Arrowtown, in Central Otago on the road from Dunedin to Queenstown is another famous gold mining town which unlike Charleston has remained virtually unchanged since its pioneer gold mining days. Our picture shows the main street asleep in the afternoon sun beneath the shelter of great trees planted by the miners a century ago. The town museum houses many relics of a period contemporary with the gold rush of California.

Top. The main street, Arrowtown.
PHOTOGRAPH, NATIONAL PUBLICITY STUDIOS

Bottom. The European Hotel, Charleston.
PHOTOGRAPH, ROBIN SMITH PHOTOGRAPHY

This striking inn sign commemorates the notorious sheep stealer James Mackenzie, and his 'Phantom Rustler' – the collie bitch that must surely have been the cleverest dog ever reared in the Southern Hemisphere. Born in Ross-shire, Scotland, about 1820, Mackenzie emigrated to Australia, and arrived in New Zealand in 1847. He sought seclusion in the unexplored mountain country of north Otago, accompanied only by his pack bullock and his collie. Having discovered a valley well below the snow line, he trained his faithful dog to cut out whole flocks of sheep from the rolling plains of Canterbury, shepherd them at night through a secret pass in the mountains into the valley, whence they were ultimately sold in the markets of the adjoining province of Otago. For more than two years Mackenzie followed the methods common enough in his native Scotland in the time of Rob Roy whose economic gospel seems to have been that 'they should take that have the power and they should keep who can', This incredible collie would accompany Mackenzie on to the plains, memorise the locality and the way back to the hills, return alone with as many as 500 sheep at a time, whilst Mackenzie would remain for the night with the shepherds and actually join in the chase for the lost flock the next day! The dog was never caught, but Mackenzie was, at last. Tried at Lyttelton in 1855 he was sentenced to 5 years imprisonment. Within the first year he had escaped and been recaptured three times and was allowed to leave the country as more nuisance than he was worth. Others tried to work the redoubtable collie, giving the orders in Gaelic as Mackenzie had done, but she would work for nobody else. For years afterwards, however, her puppies were much sought after by runholders and shepherds alike, though the record is silent as to whether her phenomenal prowess was transmitted, even within legitimate activities. The Mackenzie Country lies to the south of Lake Pukaki athwart the main highway.

Opposite
Lake Pukaki Inn Sign.
PHOTOGRAPH, ROBIN SMITH PHOTOGRAPHY

APPENDIX

The Legends
c. 950 A D

According to Maori Legends, Kupe, or Raiatea, in a seagoing outrigger canoe Matahourua, found New Zealand, circumnavigated the main islands in a figure of eight passing through Cook Strait, and returned to his people with a full account of his discoveries. Even if he had been preceded two hundred years before by the legendary Hui-te-Rangiora, Kupe's journey was one of the tremendous voyages of human adventure. Most histories accord him primacy, for remembered genealogies of a people without written record must begin somewhere in a measure of agreement.

c. 1150

Toi-te-huatahi, of Tahiti, with some of his people is said to have set out in search of his lost grandson, and was probably blown across the vast waters of Te Moana-nui-a-Kiwa to make landfall in these islands and find it already inhabited. He finally settled here, for the legends tell of one people known as Te-Tini-o-Toi, the myriads of Toi.

c. 1350

The legendary migration of many canoes, the most famous of which are Aotea, Arawa, Horouta, Mata-atua, Tainui, Takitimu, Tokomaru, and Kurahaupo, whether by chance or purposeful following of earlier sailing instructions reached Ao-tea-roa, land of the long white cloud, and settled as the main stream of subsequent Maori tradition. These early inhabitants were a peaceable people whose economy was based upon hunting the giant flightless bird, the moa. The culture of these people was different from that of the Maori when discovered by the Europeans, but it is unresolved whether this suggests more than one immigration from Polynesia.

The History
1642

Written history begins with the discovery of New Zealand by Abel Tasman in the "Heemskerck" accompanied by the "Zeehaen."

1769

Lieut. James Cook R.N. in the barque "Endeavour" led the first party of Europeans to land in New Zealand, for Tasman had been repelled by the hostility of the Maori people. Cook visited these islands five times, making his remarkably accurate charts on the first visit.

1792

Captain E. Bunker in the "William and Mary" was the first whaler to visit the new land, and in the same year two French vessels under Marion du Fresne anchored at the Bay of Islands. Du Fresne and some 28 of his party were killed and eaten by the Maori tribes for desecrating their sacred places.

1793

A visit was made to Doubtful Sound by two Spanish corvettes, and in the next ten years many vessels sought cargoes of spars, whale-oil and seal-skins.

1814

Rev. Samuel Marsden arrived at Bay of Islands bringing with him the first horses, cattle, sheep and poultry. On Christmas Day he preached the first Christian sermon in this new land.

1820

The first plough used in N.Z. by Mr.W.J.Kemp, at Keri Keri, Bay of Islands.

1823

Captain Guard commenced trading between New South Wales and New Zealand, and between 1823 and 1828 British subjects in these islands were under jurisdiction of the N.S.W. Courts of Justice.

1826

The ship "Rosanna", Captain Herd, arrived at the Bay of Islands in the first attempt at colonisation. Discouraged by conditions and the warlike manner of the natives, most of the 60 colonists left; some to settle in New South Wales, others to return to England. Only five remained in New Zealand.

1830

Rev. W. Yate brought from Sydney the first printing press to be set up in New Zealand.

1833

James Busby took up residence at Bay of Islands, the first official British Representative charged with the maintenance of law and order, but given no police force and therefore only nominal authority.

1835

First wool from New Zealand exported to Tasmania; the year that saw the visit of the famed naturalist Charles Darwin.

1839

Arrival at Port Nicholson of the ship "Tory" with the first settlers under the planning of the New Zealand Company. The land now occupied by Wellington City and suburbs was purchased. Some of the newcomers crossed to Marlborough. The 8-hour working day asserted at Petone.

1840

The first steamer in New Zealand waters; the barque "Aurora" arrived at Port Nicholson with more immi-

I

grants; and H.M.S. "Herald" brought to the Bay of Islands Captain Hobson, R.N. as Lieutenant-Governor of the Islands of New Zealand. The following month the Treaty of Waitangi was signed, ceding sovereignty by the Maori chiefs to Queen Victoria. In April, the "N.Z. Gazette" was first published in New Zealand, at Wellington; in September the Bank of New Zealand was established at Kororareka with a nominal capital of £100,000 in £10 shares; and the first overseas vessel, the barque "Platina", to enter Auckland Harbour was followed two days later by the barque "Anna Watson" carrying officials of the Government from the Bay of Islands. The Lieutenant-Governor took up residence at Auckland, and the site of the present City was purchased.

1841 New Plymouth founded and settled by immigrants from Devon and Cornwall.

1842 The first Supreme Court held at Auckland. Populations were estimated as; Wellington, 3,000; Nelson, 1,000; Wanganui, 150; other places in Cook Strait, 200. Bishop Selwyn arrived in New Zealand and preached his first sermon in the Courthouse at Auckland. Death of Governor Hobson.

1845 The first Maori War commenced in the North under Hone Heke who destroyed the town of Kororareka. Captain Grey arrived from South Australia as Lieutenant-Governor of the Colony.

1846 The New Zealand Government Act passed by the British Government and a Charter issued dividing New Zealand into New Munster and New Ulster, granting representative institutions.

1847 The first public hospital established, at Wellington.

1848 Otago founded by a Scottish Company under the auspices of the Free Church of Scotland, the "John Wycliffe" arriving at Port Chalmers with 97 immigrants, and the "Philip Laing" with 247 immigrants. In August sheep were introduced to Marlborough; and in December the first issue of "The Otago News" was published. The census of that year showed Auckland as having 4,117 houses, 137,204 cattle, 1,523,324 sheep, 14,192 horses, 122 mules and asses, 11,797 goats, 40,734 pigs. Captain Grey was appointed Governor-in-Chief over the islands of New Zealand. That part of the New Zealand Government Act of 1846 which had conferred representative institutions was suspended by Imperial Statute.

1849 The population of Dunedin and Port Chalmers was 745. In Dunedin the 8-hour system of labour was established.

1850 Foundation of Canterbury by the Canterbury Association in connection with the Church of England.

1851 The first steamship built in New Zealand, the "Governor Wynyard", launched at Freeman's Bay, Auckland; the first Mayor of Auckland appointed.

1852 The New Zealand Constitution Act passed by the British Parliament, granting self-government and dividing the country into six provinces (Auckland, Taranaki, Wellington, Nelson, Canterbury and Otago.) each with a provincial council, and a Central General Assembly set up at Auckland. In October, gold was discovered in the Kapanga Stream at Coromandel.

1854 The first New Zealand Parliament sat as the General Assembly at Auckland, opened by Lieutenant Colonel Wynyard, Administrator for the Government.

1855 The site for Invercargill township decided upon. Postage stamps were first introduced. The notorious sheep-stealer MacKenzie, after raiding the Levels run, was caught red-handed driving a thousand sheep with his redoubtable dog. The population of Otago was 2,557.

1856 On this the eighth anniversary of Otago Province its census recorded 8,854 cattle, 83,196 sheep, 854 horses May saw the appointment of the first Ministry under the system of responsible government - and its defeat a week later. The next Ministry lasted eight days. The third was more durable.

1857 The first payable goldfield in New Zealand opened at Collingwood, and the first sale of gold took place.

1858 The Province of Hawkes Bay was established in November, and in December Dr. Ferdinand von Hochstetter the famed scientist was commissioned by the New Zealand Government to make geological surveys of the Auckland and Nelson Provinces.

1859 Gold was discovered in the Buller River; Marlborough Province was established.

II

1860	The Second Maori War commenced in Taranaki; the first sale of town land was held in Oamaru.
1861	The Province of Southland was established; gold was discovered at Gabriel's Gully, Otago; a truce was made with the warring tribes in Taranaki; the first police force was organised; the first Cobb coaches began to run to the gold diggings; first issue of the "Otago Daily Times" appeared.
1862	The first regular dramatic company played at Music Hall, Dunedin; Christchurch was gazetted a municipal district; the first electric telegraph line opened (Christchurch to Lyttelton); the first direct shipment of gold was made from Dunedin to London, 15,000 ounces, public meetings "large and influential" were held in Dunedin urging separation from the North Island; two men deposited 87 pounds weight of gold in the Dunedin Treasury and declined to say where they got it; the first copy of the "Southland Times" was published in Invercargill.
1863	The first railway was opened (Christchurch to Ferrymead); Haast Pass was discovered through the Southern Alps to Westland; the Waikato Maori War began; the vessel "Helenslea" was reported to have brought a hare and half a dozen rabbits for the Southland Provincial Government; the population of Wellington was about 600.
1864	The first hansom cab reached Christchurch; Orakau pah, Waikato, was captured in memorable circumstances; gold was discovered on the West Coast of the South Island; the Intercolonial Royal Mail Company decided to run two steamers monthly between Melbourne and Auckland; Wellington was chosen as the final seat of Government and the last session of Parliament was held in Auckland.
1865	The seat of Government was removed to Wellington; Auckland was first lit by gas; a telegraph was opened between Dunedin and Invercargill and then to Christchurch; peace with the Maori tribes was proclaimed by Governor Sir George Grey; a vote in Parliament on the political separation of the two islands was 17 for, 31 against.
1867	The Thames goldfield opened; admission of four Maori members to the House of Representatives as direct representatives of the Maori people.

1868	Establishment of the County of Westland; Otago Provincial Council offered £1,500 as a bonus for the first 5,000 yards of woollen cloth locally manufactured.
1870	Extensive public works programme begins under Sir Julius Vogel; new Sydney - Auckland - San Francisco mail service announced; last detachment of the Imperial troops left the Colony.
1871	Auckland constituted a Borough (the fourth in New Zealand); municipality of Invercargill proclaimed, area 820 acres, population 1,900; inauguration of Otago University, with women allowed to attend classes and sit for examinations; manufacture of cloth commenced at Mosgiel.
1872	Formal inauguration of Saturday half-holiday, Dunedin.
1873	The 48-hour working week became law for women.
1874	Westland Province established; railway from Auckland to Otahuhu opened; under the Immigration and Public Works Policy 31,774 immigrants introduced into New Zealand. Population of Invercargill 2,400
1875	Railway from Auckland to Mercer opened; 18,324 immigrants introduced; Union Steamship Company of N.Z. established at Dunedin.
1876	Provincial governments abolished; Public Health Act passed; railway from Christchurch to Timaru opened; cable between New Zealand and New South Wales completed.
1877	Railway from Auckland carried through to Ngaruawahia; Christchurch railway carried through to Oamaru; Canterbury College and new Museum buildings opened; the Education Act passed, providing for the free and compulsory education of children.
1878	Trade unions and arbitration courts set up.
1879	Adult male suffrage introduced; the triennial Parliament Act passed.
1880	School of Agriculture (later Canterbury Agricultural College) opened at Lincoln.
1881	First telephone exchange in N.Z. opened at Woodville, and a second one at Auckland; the first crucible steel made in N.Z. at Port Chalmers.
1882	First shipment of frozen meat from New Zealand to England per "S.S. Dunedin" from Port Chalmers, shipments, 1882, 15,244 cwts. 1892, 869,600 cwts. Rotorua township sold by the Government.

1883	Auckland University College opened; telephone exchange inaugurated at Wellington; first rotary printing press introduced into N.Z.	*1906*	The N.Z. census showed a population of 888,578; the Government Advances to Workers Act passed.
1884	Horse-drawn trams commenced running in Auckland between Queen Street and Ponsonby.	*1907*	Style and designation of the Colony of New Zealand changed to Dominion of New Zealand by Royal Proclamation.
1886	Census showed Auckland's population as 64,066; Tarawera eruption and destruction of famed Pink and White Terraces with loss of 101 lives.	*1908*	The first through train, Wellington to Auckland; the Industrial Conciliation and Arbitration Amendment Act passed, abolishing Boards of Conciliation and establishing Councils of Conciliation.
1888	Electric light installed in Wellington; first freezing works in N.Z. opened at Gisborne; description published of Sutherland Falls, 1,904 feet high, fifth highest waterfall in the world; formal proclamation of British protectorate of Cook Islands.	*1909*	First recorded experiments in topdressing of land, in the Hawera district; daily express train inaugurated between Wellington and Auckland.
1891	Liberals came into power under John Ballance and later Richard Seddon introducing sweeping social and industrial legislation, commencing in September with the Land and Income Tax Assessment Act, which was followed in the next year by the first Land and Income Tax Act.	*1910*	National Provident Fund Act passed; and a Workers' Dwellings Act.
		1914	World War 1; Main Expeditionary Force left for Egypt; Western Samoa occupied by N.Z. Advance Expeditionary Force, the first enemy territory captured in the War.
1893	The Electoral Act extended the franchise to women.	*1915*	N.Z. Expeditionary Force in action on Gallipoli Peninsula.
1894	The Industrial Conciliation and Arbitration Act passed, the Land for Settlement Act authorised acquisition of private lands for settlement; the Dairy Industry Act passed for the regulation of butter and cheese manufacturing with inspection and grading for export.	*1916*	N.Z. Division transferred to Western Front.
		1919	N.Z. represented at Peace Conference; women made eligible for seats in Parliament.
		1920	N.Z. admitted to League of Nations and given mandate to administer Western Samoa; first flight over Cook Strait.
1895	The Family Homes Protection Act secured the people's homes from mortgage or sale for debt.	*1921*	N.Z. represented at Disarmament Conference.
1896	General census for the Colony showed the population as 703,360.	*1923*	Ross Dependency (Antarctica) proclaimed.
1898	Old Age Pensions Act passed.	*1928*	Kingsford Smith made first successful flight across the Tasman Sea.
1899	The first N.Z. Contingent (of ten) went to the South African War; Victoria University College, Wellington opened.	*1932*	N.Z. represented at the Ottawa Conference.
		1934	First official trans-Tasman air mail; first licensed air transport service begins.
1901	Universal penny postage adopted by N.Z.; the Cook and other Pacific islands were annexed to N.Z.; the 48-hour working week became law for men; H.M.S. "Discovery" under Captain Robert Falcon Scott sailed from Lyttleton for the Antarctic.	*1935*	Labour Government elected for first time in N.Z. the first of four successive 3-year terms.
		1936	System of guaranteed prices for butter and cheese introduced; fortyhour week becomes operative; N.Z. elected to seat on League of Nations Council.
1902	The Pacific cable opened for traffic between New Zealand, Australia, Fiji and Vancouver; the export value of frozen meat for the year was £2,718,763 and of butter and cheese £1,369,341.	*1938*	N.Z. representative elected President of the League of Nations Assembly.
		1939	Declaration of war with Germany; ships of the Royal New Zealand Navy placed under command of British Admiralty; N.Z. Air Force personnel, in R.A.F. and R.N.Z.A.F. squadrons participate in all phases of war in Europe.
1905	Old Age Pensions Act increased the annual amount to £26.		

1940	Declaration of war with Italy; first contingent of 2nd N.Z.E.F. took part in North Africa Campaign; N.Z. celebrated its centenary.	1952	Geothermal power investigations begin at Wairakei; N.Z. fighter squadron leaves for garrison air duties in Cyprus.
1941	Declaration of war with Finland, Hungary, and Rumania, and later with Japan. N.Z. Division went into action in Greece and Crete, and later took part in the second North African Campaign; R.N.Z.A.F. went into action in the Pacific area.	1953	Sir Edmund Hillary and Sherpa Tensing climb Mount Everest; armistice agreement signed in Korea; visit of H.R.H. Queen Elizabeth and Prince Philip, Duke of Edinburgh.
1942	Battle for Egypt and Alamein.	1954	N.Z. takes seat on United Nations Security Council; bulk purchase dairy contract with the United Kingdom terminated; N.Z. signs South-East Asia Treaty.
1943	End of North African campaign; N.Z. Division joins fighting in Italy; the Third Division in action against Japanese in the Solomon Islands.		
1944	Australia-New Zealand agreement providing for collaboration on matters of mutual interest; mutual-aid agreement between Canada and N.Z.	1955	N.Z. sends air force to Malaya; newsprint mills begin successful operations at Kawerau; agreement signed for reciprocal social security between N.Z. and the United Kingdom.
1945	N.Z. Division takes part in final assault in Italy; end of war in the Pacific; N.Z. joins the United Nations.	1956	Colombo Plan Conference held at Wellington; N.Z. Trans-Antarctic team and scientific party for International Geophysical Year leave for the Antarctic.
1947	The Statute of Westminster (1931) adopted by N.Z. Parliament; Prime Minister attends Japanese Peace Treaty Conference.	1957	Labour Party wins election.
		1958	Population totalled 2,315,000; Auckland 401,500; Wellington and Hutt 231,900; Christchurch 205,500; Dunedin 101,600.
1949	National Party wins election.		
1950	N.Z. represented at Colombo Conference; two N.Z. frigates and special combat force join United Nations forces in Korea; Act passed abolishing the Legislative Council (Upper House) making the House of Representatives the sole legislative body in N.Z.	1960	Superannuation benefits payable without means test from the age of 65 raised from £156 per annum to £208; in a total length of little more than a thousand miles N.Z. is served by 56,000 miles of roads, 3,500 miles of railways, 2,600 miles of regular air routes. National Party wins election.
1951	U.S.A., Australia, and New Zealand sign the ANZUS pact.	1961	Census shows total population of 2,414,064 (Maori population of 165,008).

GEOGRAPHY

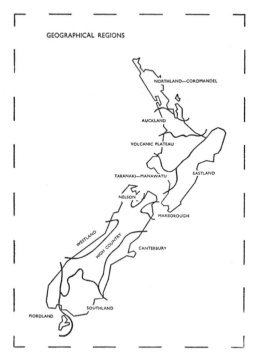

GEOGRAPHICAL REGIONS

NORTHLAND—COROMANDEL

AUCKLAND

VOLCANIC PLATEAU

TARANAKI—MANAWATU

EASTLAND

NELSON

MARBOROUGH

WESTLAND

HIGH COUNTRY

CANTERBURY

FIORDLAND

SOUTHLAND

New Zealand's nearest neighbour, Australia, is some 1,200 miles to the west; our North, South and Stewart Islands extend over a thousand miles from the sub-tropical north to almost 47 degrees south latitude where the city of Invercargill is one of the southernmost cities in the world.

New Zealand is over 103,000 square miles in area, the great majority of its people living on or near the coast.

Rainfall is generally widespread, only the districts along the eastern coast of the South Island having less than 30 inches a year. Temperatures are moderate, with clear atmosphere, bright sunshine and marked seasonal changes characteristic of the climate.

Geographically, New Zealand can be classified into eleven regions:

Northland-Coromandel: dairy farming predominant, with much hilly marginal land being developed for sheep and cattle grazing; citrus orchards and vineyards. Northland has the highest concentration of Maori population and its chief centre is Whangarei (population about 22,000).

Auckland: large population, rich pastures, ample rainfall, this region produces some 40 per cent of the country's dairy produce, half of its pig-meat and large quantities of beef, mutton and lamb, a third of the country's coal. The largest city in New Zealand, Auckland (population about 450,000) is the biggest commercial and industrial centre and the chief international shipping and airline terminal. The inland city of Hamilton (population about 50,000) and the port of Tauranga (population about 25,000) are the principal country centres.

The Volcanic Plateau: dominated by the trio of volcanic mountains, Ruapehu (9,175 feet), Ngauruhoe (7,515 feet), and Tongariro (6,458 feet), This region contains vast areas of planted forest upon which have been based timber, pulp and paper industries. Poor pumice lands are being dramatically fertilised for pasture with cobaltised superphosphate. In this area is generated the bulk of the North Island's electric power supply by a chain of hydro-electric dams along New Zealand's longest river, the Waikato, and Wairakei is notable for the only geothermal power plant in the Southern Hemisphere. Lake Taupo (239 square miles in area) is the country's largest lake and Rotorua (population about 25,000) is the main centre for the thermal regions and tourist traffic. The Tongariro National Park falls within this region.

Taranaki-Manawatu: dominated by the volcanic cone of Mount Egmont which rivals Fujiyama in its symmetry, Taranaki has high rainfall, intensive dairy farming and beautiful parks. New Plymouth (population about 33,000) and Wanganui (population about 36,000) are regional centres. To the east, the Manawatu area has mixed dairying and fat-lamb raising, with store sheep and run cattle grazed on the higher, more rugged and sparsely populated interior. Palmerston North (population about 44,000) is the thriving centre.

Eastland: Wellington is the chief city in this region. It is the capital of New Zealand and with its neighbouring city, Hutt, has a total population of about 250,000. Hawkes Bay and Poverty Bay contain about a third of New Zealand's sheep and together they are its major wool producer. On the low lands fat-lamb raising and dairying predominate, subject to the major development on the fertile river plains of cropping for the canning and quick-freezing industries. Land on the Heretaunga plains of Hawkes Bay commands up to £600 per acre for bare land, a capital cost that is moving livestock to the hills and passing the alluvial plains over to the orchards and for use in vegetable cropping for processing. The Maori population constitutes about half the rural labour force, whilst in the north-east the Maori people predominate, preserving some of the strongest Maori community traditions in New Zealand. Hastings and Napier vie for supremacy in Hawkes Bay with about 33,000 people in each city, Gisborne numbers perhaps 25,000 and Masterton about 15,000.

Nelson-Marlborough: lying at the northern end of the South Island this region enjoys the greatest number of sunshine hours in New Zealand—about 2,400 to 2,500 hours a year. The Nelson area grows all the country's tobacco and hops and a great deal of its fruit, including 40 per cent of its apples. Dairying and sheep grazing is carried on while in the Marlborough district to the east mixed cropping and livestock farming prevails. The two main centres are Nelson (population about 26,000) and Blenheim (population about 12,000).

Westland: with the highest mountain range of the Southern Alps to its east, this region receives the highest rain precipitation in New Zealand—up to 200 inches per annum in parts. Forty per cent of the country's coal and a large timber-milling industry are the main occupations. Greymouth (population about 9,000) is linked with Canterbury by rail through the 5¼ mile long Otira Tunnel beneath the Alps, which rise to over 10,000 feet and include New Zealand's highest peak, Mount Cook (12,349 feet).

The High Country: Central Otago and its surrounding districts are among the most beautiful areas in New Zealand, notably in the autumn when the cold temperatures work their wizardry with trees and foliage. Rugged and sparsely populated, it is the area for fine wools on large sheepruns of up to 10,000 acres. In the more sheltered and sunny basins of Central are stone-fruit orchards and small pockets of mixed cropping and livestock farming. The snowfields, mountains, glaciers and many magnificent lakes provide scenic and sporting attractions, quite apart from the special character of the people themselves—among the friendliest in New Zealand. In the south are a number of hydro-electric dams, including the country's largest at Roxburgh on the Clutha River.

Canterbury-North Otago: here lies the largest plain in the country, with mixed cropping and livestock farming producing 80 per cent of New Zealand's wheat, 75 per cent of its barley, and 57 per cent of the oats. Short-term pastures, with fat lambs and sheep are rotated with the crops. Rainfall being low, irrigation is widely used. Christchurch, New Zealand's third city in size (population about 220,000) dominates this region and in many respects Westland also; but Timaru on the coast (population about 27,000) and Oamaru (population about 13,000) are thriving farming and manufacturing centres. Ashburton (population about 12,000) is the chief town of mid-Canterbury and its associated country is known as the granary of New Zealand.

Southland-East Otago: the lowlands and downlands feature fat-lamb production and fodder crops, while to the south lies some of the finest dairying land in the country, with extensive sheep-grazing in the hills, and major limeworks to augment the superphosphate which maintains fertility in the leached-soil areas. The city of Dunedin (population about 105,000) has an influence far greater than its numbers would suggest, rooted both in its past as the chief financial centre of the Dominion and in its present status as the city with a medical and dental school as part of its University. Invercargill, rapidly-growing centre of Southland has a population of about 42,000 and is developing its port at Bluff as a major outlet for the rich inland production.

Fiordland-Stewart Island: this region is the tourist's own; with Fiordland's unrivalled lakes and sea-inlets, mountains and sounds, forests and river-valleys. Sparsely populated, isolated and rugged, this unique area is well served with tourist resorts and planned expeditions by road, water and airway sightseeing. Stewart Island has a special place in the New Zealander's affections as the country's main supplier of oysters.

THE NATIONAL PARKS

The National Parks movement is one of the happier inventions of the United States and one that New Zealand has enthusiastically adopted. A nation that can boast over ten million members of its national Forest and Bird Protection Society, millions more enrolled in its Audubon Society and that can attract half its nearly two hundred million citizens to its National Parks merits emulation.

New Zealand has constituted eight National Parks containing about one-seventeenth of its central islands' area; chiefly mountains, forests and rugged coastal country, retained in unspoiled natural beauty for the pleasure of all who would visit them. Wildlife and natural vegetation flourish there in undisturbed solitude.

The tourist will find himself in the heart of three or four of our National Parks as he visits the more famous beauty spots in both Islands; the others must be sought out for their own sake.

Urewera National Park: Eastward of the thermal regions of Rotorua and forming the catchment basin of Lakes Waikaremoana and Waikareiti, 120,000 acres of the heaviest native bush in the North Island comprise an area dark with bloody tribal history. The campaigns against the famous Maori rebel chief, Te Kooti, centred for several years in these mountain fastnesses, where the old fox kept a resident British force pinned down in exasperation as he exploited every resource of this precipitous and often impenetrable country. The gorge road from Murupara to the Lake Tourist Hotel at Waikaremoana is memorable, and at journey's end is excellent accommodation with angling in season. This route takes the traveller from the north through the eastern province of Hawke's Bay, which itself is like ten thousand acres of English deer park; and swings south through the Manawatu Gorge to Palmerston North and the main road to Wellington.

Tongariro National Park: If the traveller chooses the central route from north to south of the North Island, visiting Rotorua and Taupo, he will be tempted to stay at the Chateau Tongariro Tourist Hotel. His first sight in the foyer is a memorial bust of Chief Te Heuheu, who was responsible for the gift to the nation of the sacred mountain peaks which dominate Tongariro National Park— Mounts Ruapehu, Tongariro and Ngauruhoe— each more or less an active volcano. Standing sufficiently remote to constitute no hazard to life or property, these volcanic peaks—particularly Ngauruhoe— are spectacular in their periodic eruptions. It is the fond hope of all visitors that from the grandstand site of the Chateau the mountain will perform in full majesty—plumed with emitted cloud by day, aglow by night. In the summit basin of Ruapehu lies Crater Lake,

steaming hot amidst perpetual ice and snow. When Ruapehu erupted in 1954-56 this lake disappeared temporarily. It is likely to be there to reward the climber.

Facilities for snow-sports on these mountains are amongst the best in New Zealand, with chair-lifts, tow-bars and an alpine village maintained by ski-clubs. The Chateau is a perfect base for one of our best national parks.

Egmont National Park: Lying to the west of the main route south, and still in the North Island, the Taranaki province is one of the country's richest dairying districts. Mount Egmont bestrides it like the famed Japanese Mount Fujiyama, symmetrical, snow-capped and affording three accommodation houses from any of which the visitor enjoys a tremendous panorama of country-side as gravid as the Cotswolds, lush with pasture sustained by the rainfall precipitated by Egmont's soaring peak.

One of the most easily accessible of all our National Parks, Egmont repays those who like to stand and stare at nature all benign.

Abel Tasman National Park: Now we are in the South Island, whose rugged northern coastline so intrigued the early navigators. The Dutchman for whom this Park is named, sailed through Cook Strait (as it was later named) and the surveyor d'Urville charted its coves and headlands. This park is a tramper's and camper's preserve, and can be penetrated only so far, by road from the Takaka district, or by launch cruise along the coast behind which Pelion piles upon Ossa in mountain ranges that are the sunniest in all New Zealand.

Nelson Lakes National Park: In this mountainous area of wooded valleys lie the source lakes of the Buller River—Rotoiti and Rotoroa. The visitor should note in his diary the spellings of Maori names for the North Island also has a lake Rotoiti and a Lake Rotorua; here we are in the South Island in another unsophisticated play-ground for the tramper and mountaineer, the skier and trout fisherman.

Arthur's Pass National Park: The surrounding country passes in review from the trans-alpine road from east to west; from Canterbury to Westland, at some 3,000 feet through the Southern Alps, flanked by mountain ranges of 7,000 feet and upwards. Going by rail, the visitor plunges through the divide by the famed Otira Tunnel, among the twelve longest in the world. This is alpine country comparable in every respect to the Austrian Tyrol and the famed passes of Switzerland.

VIII

Mount Cook National Park: Here are our loftiest peaks—17 of them exceeding 10,000 feet, with Mount Cook itself (12,349 feet) the most photographed peak in the Southern Hemisphere. The Tasman Glacier can be negotiated in parts of its 18-mile length by even the most sedentary visitor to the Mount Cook Hermitage Hotel, and for the lover of the strenuous life there are major ski-grounds and mountaineering to daunt the hardiest. The tourist can scarcely escape the claims of Mount Cook, for it is one of our inexhaustible talking points.

Fiordland National Park: By the simple expedient of taking this course from north to south of New Zealand we have kept the best wine till the last. Description of Fiordland is strictly a matter for the superlatives department. Nearly three million acres of the most complete and breathtakingly varied natural splendour await the visitor however he journeys—by rail or landliner, rental car or aircraft; vistas of alpine mass and forested valley, lakes and rivers and waterfalls (the Sutherland Falls are the fifth highest in the world). Hunter or fisherman, tramper or mountaineer, or just plain sight-seer collecting memories, Fiordland offers you Nature at its most majestic and magnificent.

These then are New Zealand's National Parks in briefest outline. The visitor will wisely turn to the admirable Government Tourist literature for more worthy description.

THE NEW ZEALAND PEOPLE

The total population is about two and a half million, of which some 165,000 are Maoris. There are further populations in the Cook Islands (about 18,000), Niue (about 5,000), and the Tokelau Islands (about 2,000), all of which are New Zealand territories. All of these island peoples are Polynesians.

More than two-thirds of the people of New Zealand live in the North Island, a reversal of the early settlement period of the 19th century. Industry and manufacturing in the north have throughout this century drawn the population away from the South Island. Just over half the population lives in the 18 main urban centres of the country and some 65 per cent in all live in towns and cities.

Settled mainly by British people who for the most part came directly from the United Kingdom, immigration has been in this century a less important factor in population growth than natural increase, which accounts for some three-quarters of the total annual gain. In the year ended March 31st 1959 migration totalled 10,000, and over the previous decade some 105,000. Assisted immigrants have been brought to New Zealand at the rate of 5,000 a year, but this number has now been reduced to about 3,300, selected on the basis of age, occupation and available accommodation. They undertake to work in approved occupations for a limited period, and are drawn almost wholly from the United Kingdom, though some have come from the Netherlands under a special agreement with the Government of that country. Over 4,500 displaced persons from Europe came out under an agreement with the former International Refugee Organisation, and in 1956 and 1957 over a thousand refugees from Hungary came to New Zealand.

The number of births has been steadily rising, and since 1950 has been about 26 per 1,000 of population. The infant mortality rate is some 22 deaths per 1,000 births, the expectation of life is over 68 years for men and over 72 years for women. The rate of increase of the Maori people is between 3 and 4 per cent per annum, one of the highest rates in the world. The birthrate—46 per 1,000 population—makes for a young population and over 60 per cent of the Maori people are under 21 years of age. About a third of the Maoris now live in cities and towns.

The average age of New Zealanders is between 30 and 31 years, so that by comparison with the age structure of other countries New Zealand has a high proportion of children and young people, somewhat low proportions of middle years, and a moderate ratio of older people from 60 years on. Some 47 per cent of New Zealanders are under 25 years of age, 41 per cent between 25 and 59, and 12 per cent over 60 years of age.

In the typical New Zealand family there are two or three young children; of the male popula-tion about 56 per cent are actively engaged in industry, and of the female population less than 20 per cent are in industry.

The main religious professions are approximately; Church of England 36 per cent; Presbyterian 22 per cent; Roman Catholic 14 per cent; Methodist 8 per cent.

PRIMARY INDUSTRY

Most of New Zealand's 43,200,000 acres of occupied agricultural and pastoral land and much of its high country, is devoted to sheep and cattle grazing. There are more owners than employees on our farms, an important factor in the very high level of farm productivity. Some 8,000,000 acres of pasture are top-dressed with fertilizer each year, the agricultural aviation industry covering one-third of this area.

Two University Agricultural Colleges, Lincoln College and Massey College provide scientific and technical training, carry out sustained research, and graduate enough young farmers to maintain New Zealand as the most highly advanced farming country in the world. The Departments of Agriculture and Scientific and Industrial Research conduct demonstration farms and research stations of the greatest importance.

Wool is sold on the free world market, and producers, with their own funds, provide a guaranteed minimum return for growers each season. Dairy produce and meat are marketed through producer organisations, chiefly because of the special problems in this field for a country whose markets are in distant lands. The New Zealand producer organisations have proved highly efficient in their marketing practices.

High country farms specialising in wool production favour the hardy Merino sheep; the more fertile lowland farms carrying up to six sheep to the acre look more to the production of lamb and mutton. South Island fattening farms carry many Corriedale sheep, New Zealand's own dual-purpose breed. Romneys, however, are the most important breed, representing some 63 per cent of the total sheep population of over 47,000,000. So efficient is the wool industry that although New Zealand is only fourth in the world in sheep population, it is the third largest wool producer and the second largest wool exporter.

New Zealand is the largest exporter in the world of mutton and lamb, accounting for three-quarters of total world exports. Most of these exports are to the United Kingdom. Beef production has been chiefly a by-product of sheep farming, with cattle grazing surplus grass and fern, then fattened on better pasture; though it is also increasingly associated with dairying under the stimulus of improved overseas demand. Dairying is carried on mainly in the North Island, in districts where a well distributed and ample rainfall maintains pastures of the highest quality. The mild climate of New Zealand renders the winter housing of cattle unnecessary.

Of the 2,000,000 dairy cows in milk in New Zealand, 85 per cent are Jerseys, most of them proven herds from long-term scientific breeding programmes. Butter and cheese are the major products with processed milk increasing, and casein variable according to world demand.

Grain growing is on a small scale and chiefly for local consumption though improving prices may encourage further development in this field of agriculture. Two-thirds of the grain comes from Canterbury, where it is often worked in rotation with fat-lamb production.

Most of the country's orchards are located in the sunny, dry areas of Hawkes Bay, Nelson and Central Otago; apples being the chief export crop. New Zealand's own canning industry has made the country self-sufficient in all vegetables and most fruits, and the quick-frozen food industry ranks with that of the United States in per capita consumption—far ahead of any other British country.

SECONDARY INDUSTRIES

Over the past quarter-century, employment in factories has more than doubled, and is now 25 per cent of the country's labour force; factory production too has more than doubled, the wage-bill has increased five-fold and the value of production six-fold.

One person in every five working in New Zealand depends directly on manufacturing for his or her livelihood; one-quarter of the 160,000 working in factories are women and girls. This excludes the servicing trades. Auckland has 30 per cent of all factory workers; the other three main cities account between them for another 37 per cent, leaving about a third of the total number scattered about the country. This is of course a most uneven spread of manufacturing industry dictated by New Zealand's pattern of a few highly concentrated urban areas. Four out of every five women factory workers are in one or other of these four main cities.

This emphasises the classic problem of human concentration. Quite apart from the effect in the few main centres of the growing complexities of services and accommodation, the lack of future employment for youth in the smaller towns and cities requires a strong policy of industrial location in future expansion.

New Zealanders produce and process nearly all their own food; our woollen goods and blankets are renowned and the bulk of our clothing needs are met by our factories using both domestic and imported materials; nearly all footwear and hosiery is made locally and many of our leather goods. Well established light foundries and precision engineering works build locomotives, small ships, coach bodies and mechanical plant for factory production. The electrical industries are now well diversified, from light bulbs to batteries, radios and radiators, wires and cables, domestic refrigerators and vacuum cleaners. Seventy per cent of New Zealand homes have electric washing machines, 65 per cent have refrigerators and nearly 50 per cent have vacuum cleaners—the greater part of all these appliances being of local manufacture.

Rubber production depends upon imported raw material, but makes tyres, tubes, and every domestic article in the range. Plastics, paints furniture and fabrics are all produced in our factories, and items like chemicals, soap and cosmetics, pottery and glassware can be included in the list. Where components are necessarily imported, such as with motor vehicles, many of which are assembled in New Zealand, then the main industrial objective is to increase the final value of the product to the maximum by the use of local labour for assembly and finishing.

New Zealand is a moderate tariff country, and upwards of half of its imported goods enter free of duty. The tariff policy is based upon three requisites; the need for revenue, protection of some local industries, and the support of Commonwealth trade. The highest duties are on semi-luxury imports such as alcoholic spirits, tobacco, and motor spirits, this latter being the least defensible of all in an expanding industrial economy so dependent upon transport whose costs are among the highest in the world. The greater part of the total customs revenue collected in New Zealand arises from the foregoing three items.

Practically all imports from the United States and other dollar area countries come under the import licensing procedure which has been in operation for many years in one form or another to maintain a reasonable balance of trade and payments within the dollar area. Despite these restrictions, nearly two-fifths of the goods available in New Zealand are imported from other countries, and our factories must continue to rely upon overseas countries for most of their heavy machinery and for much of their raw materials, such as iron, steel, and aluminium. Major projects are afoot to correct this dependence by the establishment of iron and aluminium rolling and smelting plants.

INDEX

INDEX

(This index does not include the *appendix*)

References to illustrations in italic

Printed by
E. S. & A. Robinson (N.Z.) Ltd.
Auckland

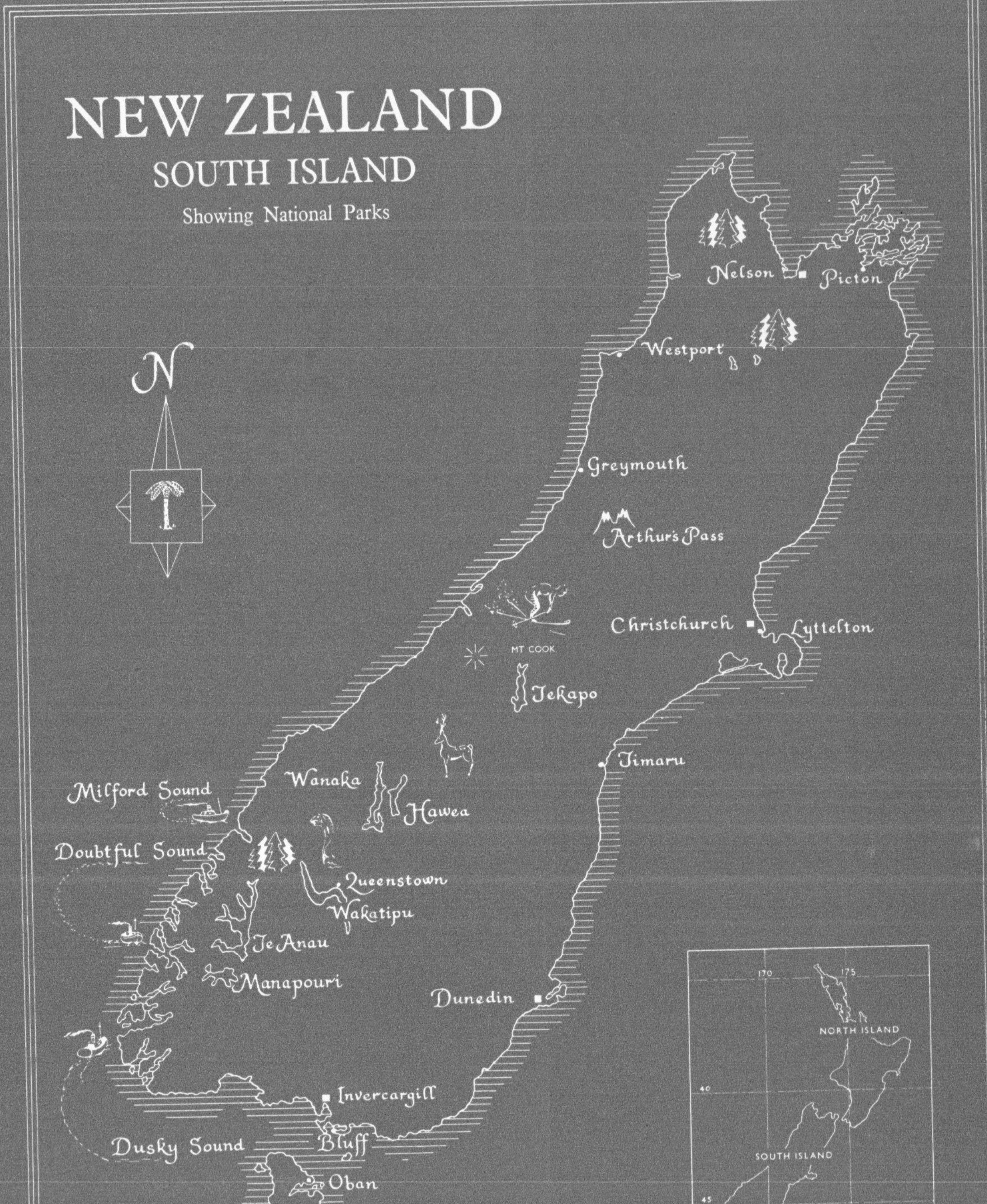
NEW ZEALAND
SOUTH ISLAND
Showing National Parks
N
Nelson
Picton
Westport
Greymouth
Arthur's Pass
Christchurch
Lyttelton
MT COOK
Tekapo
Timaru
Wanaka
Hawea
Milford Sound
Doubtful Sound
Queenstown
Wakatipu
Te Anau
Manapouri
Dunedin
Invercargill
Dusky Sound
Bluff
Oban
STEWART ISLAND
170
175
NORTH ISLAND
40
SOUTH ISLAND
45